Keir Hardie Street

Keir Hardie Street

Alan Morrison

Published 2010 by
Smokestack Books
PO Box 408, Middlesbrough TS5 6WA
e-mail : info@smokestack-books.co.uk
www.smokestack-books.co.uk

Keir Hardie Street
Alan Morrison

Cover image: Alan Morrison, from a photograph provided by
Step Back in Time, 25 Queens Road, Brighton BN1 3WB

Printed by
EPW Print & Design Ltd

ISBN 978-0-9560341-6-8
Smokestack Books gratefully
acknowledges the support of
Arts Council England

LOTTERY FUNDED

Smokestack Books is
represented by Inpress Ltd
www.inpressbooks.co.uk

With the abolition of private property ... we shall have true, beautiful, healthy Individualism. Nobody will waste his life in accumulating things, and the symbol for things. One will live. ... Most people exist, that is all ... It will be a marvellous thing — the true personality of man — when we see it. It will grow naturally and simply, flower-like, or as a tree

(Oscar Wilde, *The Soul of Man Under Socialism*)

Sure, the lovely fools who made Utopia
Planned it without any aspidistra.
There will be a heaven on earth, but first
We must banish from the parlour
Plush and poker-work...

(Harold Monro, 'Aspidistra Street')

For like a mole I journey in the dark,
A-travelling along the underground
From my Pillar'd Halls and broad Suburbean Park,
To come the daily dull official round...

(John Davidson, 'Thirty Bob a Week')

Fill your house with what is beautiful and useful.

(William Morris)

...any good of which human nature is capable has to be revealed, since what is shown to be practicable must be put into practice

(Pelagius)

I shall be satisfied when I awake.

(*Psalm 17*)

Contents

Keir Hardie Street

I Whittington's City

Gash of grubby blood-brick buildings
Congealed under a bandaged sky
In every doily-curtained window heaves a life —
Motionless stout spectators crouch, watch the trains snail in,
Black bricks of Battersea do the steam proud,
Steeplejack chimneys tousle to attention,
Colobus clouds swing from chimney to chimney:
A belching audience stirred fresh from choked beds,
First fags of the day plume from drainpipe-brimmed trilbies.

Tock-o-clock in the morning, too early to tell the time; 10
Through ghoulish fogs peeling back like greying scabs
The city pricks up higgledy-piggledy against Calvary skyline:
A pencil-rub of pea-souped rooftops bruising on the paper arm
Of the street urchin pale, pearly horizon —
Soon brushed away by the charlady sun.

Ash-mouthed London — a chimneysweep's lung,
Charred and catarrhed, spluttering soot, black
Tubercular blood: a broom-thumped rug's
Muddy dyes running in the slurries of the slums
—Guttersnipe city; barely the puff 20
For a thought to splutt up a sputumed verb,
Clogged as smoggy zephyrs through
Honeycombs of gap-toothed stucco,
Ochre as plaque-caked screeching teeth
Of Jack-stalked slatterns, flapping down the
Daisy—Daisy—airless backstreets
With asthmatic, *Lambeth Walk*, music hall swag;
A lost panting tramp in labyrinth pitch,
Ginned to the skin, a proppa' Cockney sparra'
Bow-legged and belled, barrelling out his 30
Roll out the Barrels as he Rag-And-Bones by.

II Short Shanks the Shopkeeper

On Arcadia Street, Old Short Shanks Joe
Stirs to the salts of his wife's soapy hands
Offering a Rosy Lee libation
Steaming sweet n' piping brown
As the Ganges in Kiplin's In'ja —
Rushed sips and kippers, crockery clanks;
Slap of lather for junket-thick shave,
Scrape, scrub, scrape, scrub, scrub-a-dub-dub —
Punctual as tulips is this old Buff — 40
Time to puff up n' peel on his slippers,
Flip-flop and trip down the apples and pears,
Lift up the shutters of the shut-eye shop —
Hosiery, drapery, haberdasher, colliboshe r—
Sharp as a radish in his Piccadilly collar,
Time to butter up more bread and honey
With a *Knees up Mother Brown* and a bish, bash, bosh!

Polishes his clobber, spanking dapper for *Daisy* day,
All manner of hats, all shapes and spats,
Whistles *My Old Man's a Dustman* as 50
His hoarded goods dust up spick and spam;
Old Joe only takes notes crisp from the franking,
No credit or slates in his kind of banking —
Coughed his way up from a draper's fag,
Chores of a poor slopshop h'appren'ice,
To flush haberdasher with a ledger for saving —
Scrimped, scraped, scrubbed for this crust of a chance
To pass to his sons all his scrimpings and scrapings.

Long ago when Shanks was just a wistful titch
In shorter hoes, mince pies glitter-bright and life- 60
-is-but-a-dream-blue, he filled this dismal city
With laughter parting jackdaw-cawing avenues,
Taking the wind, filth and laundry with him,
Lifting the fogs of old Tobacco Dock,
The smog of lung-chugged tugs, tarred sails
Of junks n' clippers, kippers' scaly tails

Flappin' in the mustardy yella' cha shalla's,
The whiffs from Canary Wharf's hot chestnut sellers,
The oranges-and-lemons of St. Paul's pealin' 'eavens,
The lugubrious gongs of galumphing Big Ben — 70
Blew them up in a paper bag and burst them!

So full of big 'n' brassy, band-stand grand ideas,
Fishing possibilities in the ditchwater-green
Time-pummelled lustre of his twitching Thames,
A quixotic chevalier's rusty armour:
The city's next Dick Whittington, rags-to-riches
Row-row-row-your-boat rise to power,
And with that power, O what mighty deeds:
He'd level this topsy-turvy city —
So tramps have more attentive tailors, 80
Slums 'n' lean-tos fill with life and laughter,
Churches over-brim with the penitent rich
Soliciting forgiveness with flag-scraping prayers
Till their camel humps shrank needle-size
Back into their farthing-nabbing eyes;
Shopkeepers, landlords, all offering alms
To the downtrodden last; ill-gotten profits
Put back in bellies of cash-strapped customers,
No more cap-in-hand — now slate-in-gait…
He'd gallop up the wooden hill to Bedaffordshire 90
Each pinking night to map his piping dreams,
Architect of air-castles, cartographer fantastical
Planting striding vistas arced by apple trees
Vast enough for citizens to amble hand-in-hand
From Pimlico to Chelsea, in a ripe Republic Land.

But something struck him while he eyed the rungs
Of his mind's assembling ladder: *What if,*
H'instead of taking this 'ere beanstalk to the chop
I stops right 'ere, makes me pitch, h'n' opens up a shop?
With a fee fie fiddle-fum, he slaps dann' a deposit 100
On a knackers-yard's narked carcass he guts n' furnishes
With the h'energy n' h'enterprise of a scrub of whirling Dervishes,
N' all the h'oriental lustre his Boxer mitts can muster,
Then throws his spanking premises a fancy awning-wide for trade,

Makes himself a hagglers' patch, a market tailor-made
For his clothier's chalk talents, a dapper haberdasher's
Hats and spats for strutting Hares of Fashionable Society,
Spangled goods aglow, gold cufflinks, green carnations,
Best grey serge la Camel Corps, plaid lapels, wool blazers,
Spongee, duck and seersucker, SHANKS' best-twilled brand 110
To send Bespoke tags all a-twitch, and Savile Row a-slavering...

In time he polishes his golden nest-egg all a-razz,
Sells it on, then architects his brick-and-mortar castle,
All turrets, regal mouldings, then sets to work to profit
On the profits from his profits, shore up shares and capital
Like dazzled Mister Kipps, but still promising his soul
He'll not forget the sweat he scrubbed up from,
Nor his cloth of promise, why he had begun this:
To share his surplus loaves among the starved,
The cash-strapped, dispossessed, the workhouse mice — 120
But before he sets to this bold transformation
Of his slum-sunken, broken-spirit city,
He needs-must bake enough dough to raise it up a crust,
N' no van-flagging dilly-dallying on the way.

But when the day comes he's got enough to spare,
Married with three nippers, a fourth'n on the way,
Up to his bally armpits in draperies and prams,
Such a busy-bees' knees, pays two boys a pittance
To run his rag-shop for him while he gains weight and cigars,
In his fez to rival Khartoum Gordon, n' 'andlebar moustache 130
To out-kit cartouche Kitchener; flush with all blinkin' manner
Of sundry accoutrements, brand spanking penny-farthing
N' a dapper twenty carat fob-watch engraved with 'is h'initials —
An old cork-'elmet Pasha in Sudan E14 —
Comfy cushion salon days plotting stovepipe schemes
To expand 'is little h'empire, swell its bounteous borders —
Incorporate more shops, more boys, more trade,
But most of all make sure that nothing's given
Without a profit's promise of Return —
Trouble with Robin Hood, thinks Joe, he had no Knowledge, 140
No business h'acumen — I must shore up me' profits,
Moth-ball my wads of Capital, lift me' h'offspring up
To a better level than the filthy slum-hass' what I sprouted from!

The city, his Old China, spittle-thick with kith,
Spits of Shankses numbering from Spitalfields to Tooting Beck,
But who'd favour cousins, poor relations, over closer kin?
'E'd do 'is h'apenny bit for the pond-life hoi polloi —
But 'is h'empire's sun must never set, must pass to his first son
Per primogen-h'iture (what's good enough for h'Empress Goose...)
To build on it in turn for *his* own dustbin lids, 150
A dynasty of Shankses, though one with common touch
And nostalgia for their downtrodden origins
But buttered into dreams of self-betterment and creams
As anthracite Disraeli's Marble Angels
Sculpted out of labours' noble brows, pooled back into
Alms-doling Charity to inflate the Church's coffers;
Soot-foot orphans parish-sponsored to shadow Steeple
Sweepers; damp tramps handed palm-dry pairs of togs;
Charladies glissading with chaperoning mops;
Wreathes made from lilies-of-the-gutter laid on 160
Jumble-humped camels of rag-and-bone carts
Trailed by processions of soup-kitchen aprons
Dispensing baptisms of gin, gloop and broth —
All this generosity to be ladled out by Me:
I'll patent it Short Shanks's Charity!

What has become of Short Shanks since?
He's prospered, passed on through the needle's eye
Across Thames' littered Styx to Heaven's Pillar'd Halls —
His kith and kin keep building, stacking high,
Lost scope some moons ago with common ground 170
Of microscopic internecine conflicts,
Battalions of ants battling for leafy scraps,
Divided citizens who've lost sight of the sky
For marble towers blotting it from view; draping high
From scaffoldings, like a giant's laundry out to dry,
Hoardings of hackneyed banner-legends fly:
YOU TOO CAN SCALE THESE HEIGHTS IF YOU GRIT YOUR NOSE TO THE GRINDSTONE — PROFIT AS YOU'D NOT BE PROFITED BY!
STASH YOUR FOUR AND TWENTY BLACKBIRDS IN THE RIGHT PIE!

III Three True Obscuritans

— The Hermit of Hercules Buildings

Once heard tales of an unfashionable recluse 180
Hid like a fiend in the icinged wedge
Of Hercules Buildings (his visioning spied
As a future pub called *The Pineapple*) —
Then Molton Street, where he swore blind
He met Mephistopheles on the stairs;
A hermitage of thirty years or more,
Never itching to twitch his curtains to spy
Inspiration in people-bustled streets, *his*
Was in-spiriting, in-growing: those oyster lids
Closed daily to part the lobed clouds of his head, 190
Gifting insights into all gilded things,
Graven and engraving, visions of lost Albion,
Jerusalem's grass growing in the grime of gin-fumed streets
And airless—*Daisy*—alleyways; emerald wisteria
Crawling dirt-abraded walls, hankering after sunlight
As thinkers clawing at the truth — a Gravesend Eden
Of crumbled chimneystacks, rampant vines and seething
Creepers choking porticos, architraves of Inigo's,
His vaults to masques of blackness, glorious green-
Blemishing of gorgonzola marble, carrageen 200
Ruins of raised Atlantis, a Classical Capital's
Rubble sprung with shrubs and arbutus, felled columns'
Trampled mushroom stumps in billows of blooming trees.

They say 'Batty' Mister Blake rarely left his digs,
Save by night, consulting angels on Peckham Rye —
His Old Dutch brang him round in dismal mornings
With a cup of warm and wet, reading the daily
Tea-leaves verbatim to his Milton mesmerised
By a flea's ghost on her shoulder — as that foggy-eyed
Artist after sunstroke, by tones of absent sitters — 210
Imparting obscure prophecies; nothing imbibed
But tobacco and Souchong by this Lambeth Shaman —
Thirty years with curtains drawn so light from within

Could burst un-assuaged; no noise but the squeak
Of his press inspiriting into print his singing lines
Impressed ever since on our mimicking minds —
Why should one who strides with Angels care
Whether his works see daylight; succumb
To hand-grabs of grubbing publishers?
Better to be damned in one's own imprint, 220
Let the flyleaves calcify like gossamer membranes,
Smudge to brass-rubbings under autumn's thumb.

— *The Turpentine Prophet*

I've a dream-fired friend, a struggling writer, pure
Spit and spirit, distemper and turpentine,
Can't get his novel published 'cause editors won't read it
Unless the manuscript is put in type —
He's got Socialism thumping in his heart
N' rumbling like a thunder in his belly,
But for all his revolutionary fervour,
He still must bow his knees to earn a crust — 230
As he does for the unleavened on his Sundies —
Eighteen hour days painting walls of betters,
Plastering and filling up the cracks,
While like-ravines ravage his scamped hands
Chiselling his phizog with fatigue —
A messianic journeyman with cultured sensibilities
Reduced to scrimping from menial means
A second coat of matt Utopianism —
A lumpen skidder, neither Upstairs nor Downstairs,
But balanced on Class's banisters: Midstairs; 240
His workmates strip him down a peg or two,
Their penny dreadful shell-likes just won't listen —
Prefer to scamp their makeshift trestle lives
Slopping shoddy bricks of their own prison,
Slaking on stout, plastered as Paris;
Placing depleting pennies on deceptive bets,
Slaving to keep themselves in bread and cigarettes —
No thoughts on fighting for the right of labour
To employ their souls and minds as well as bodies;
No burning desire in their turpentine hearts 250

To rent sublime swirls, twirling intricacies
Of flora on wallpaper they slop and paste
To peel and blister: the patterns of waste.

— *The Ghost of a Poet*

Another friend, or should say the ghost of one,
Suffered much, swallowed pride's stale crust,
Him and his flint-and-roses missus
Love on empty tums n' all a-pother,
Something borrowed bond, and something blue,
Doing without for scrimped months at a time
So's he could turn his poverty to poetry — 260
Little in the two words after all but a 'v' —
Before his callused hands puffed up from graft to grip
Something as gentlemanly as a pen; let's not forget,
A tool more suited to the mitts of better furnished men.
—And was it worth it? Yes, each bitter, bleeding line;
But meagre recognition of tepid-inked reviews
Was scarce enough to save him from his cancer fancies, so
He hurled himself from off a Cornish cliff when in Penzance
Taking his 'cure', a poet in his prime of death, a Hippo-
Posthumous besotted by his own h'obituary; 270
Left his flinty trouble-and-strife sixty bob in savings,
Double what they'd ingeniously eke
On an average, tummy-grumbling week,
Him jarred by a hack's asthmatic stubs
In the pubs and rubs of Grub Street.

— *Those Intractable Art Martyrs*

Only hope of recognition for their paper labours,
Posthumous, I'll bet you, it'll come
Decades down the Circle line of time,
Long past their unmarked paupers' graves as nameless
As that old Tommy Anonymous's tomb 280
Who got it in the cork from a Dervish poking fork
Squared-in on all sides by Fuzzy Wuzzy whirligig —
Leave ghosted legacies in inner-city cemeteries,
No towering memorials to soldiers of the pen and brush,

No carrara Marble Arch to salute their funeral march;
Only those whose shell-likes catch the pealing chimes
And clamouring cries of spiritual picket-lines —
Pearly Bow Bells of the other side —
To witness their mute protests, blank placards,
Haunting that grubby Abbey with spectral petitions 290
To be with the Remembered in that Corner —
A Purgatory of posthumous spectating
After gritty lifetimes scraping paper scraps
In hacking garrets, buckling flophouses,
Consumptive slums, ammonic coffeehouses,
Cramped backyards' hackneyed dominackers,
Ditch-stinking prisons of non-recognition
(Castes away from the miniature literatures
Of Fitzrovia's portico'd icing-stuccoed streets);
The Ganges of Moorfields; Obscurity's Scrubs; 300
Or worse: a parchment-dry critic's drubs.

What foiled their immortality? Did they wordsmith in vain?
Their words were the same as those the better-placed
Poets used to compose their celebrated verses;
Their pens scratched paper as visibly, as musically
And noisily as those from whom we've heard —
So how come they didn't join them into print?
Because they craved a more discerning press
Sympathetic to their garret struggles,
Plaster-scraped patois and woodchip lingos, 310
Not bucolic idylls typed by lily-white Literati,
Published prompt by prized imprints to patronage and puffery.

How, short of shouting out crimson sedition
Like that Moses-bearded German from
The amplified pulpit of Speakers' Corner,
Could socialists scrimp crusts of consolation
From dead-ends of mundane minds? Nagging
Conviction: *It IS possible* — so Lilburne and Walwyn
Proselytised; Everard and Winstanley set digging
Its foundations, planting crops in absented Broadsides 320
Of grabbed lands — their cause, decamped at spiked Putney
Before it bloomed: the trounce of shining Ironsides

Tramping their light to embers in Buckinghamshire;
The Chartists and the Unions marched under its banner;
Phossy-jawed and balding match-girls hatched tactical strikes
Catching fast to apparatchiks of its Dockers' Tanner;
Morris wove and wallpapered with fabric from its grain,
Printed the *Commonweal*, Worship Street's loss-making gain;
Blatchford launched the *Clarion* to cite its Christian links;
Its baton passed to Lansbury's 'miracle of Fleet Street', 330
The ha'penny *Herald*; then the *Citizen* — truth as cheap
As chips but unadulterated by the gutter grease...

Keir Hardie infused its inspiration to exact
Leveret leaps and bounds of a dauntless autodidact
To a dumbstruck Commons, stalking tortoise to Etonians,
Ambushing Oxford Blues slumbered on green benches
Of old St. Stephens, disarming arguments with roar of lions
Through filibustering lobbies, pettifogs of smoking-rooms —
Standard-bearer of a new breed, by hand and by brain,
Cradle to grave; Workhouse Crooks' Tory Woolwich gain; 340
Their triumphs over low origins might have sooner reaped
Industry's ripe fruits had suffrage's swelling numbers
Amassed to the cause as fast as taking invitations
To Mr. Pease's easy parties of teapot politics
Where Mr. Quintus Fabius poured sugared gradualness
Into Cunctator crockery on rustling service trays —
Idle silver singers of fancy cake-stand days —
But for a torch-browed gatecrasher who saw beautiful things
Through glass coffee infusers of Lotus-eating tiffins.

IV The Sea-Green Line

I commuted along the City and South London; 350
Not retreating, digressing, a mental pilgrimage
In electric-flickered carriage underground
To find new perspectives on the glum city above,
Alighted at the ghost station of my haunted conscience
In shadows of Progress' echoing tomb…
Followed the stations on the curved roof carriage:
MOORGATE…OLD STREET…ANGEL….KING'S CROSS…

Hours clattered by; I soon found myself dazed
On a sepulchral platform whose designated name
Had yet to be assigned — lost, I stumbled blind 360
Through combing catacombs, labyrinthine tunnels
Circling tile-scaled burrow walls, till I tripped onto
Another nameless platform, un-haunted by commuters —
Then out the char-black mouth of the howling tunnel,
The elephantine roar of an approaching behemoth
Screeching into view on the scuffed track's trailing tongue
From out the tunnel's mouth — a metallic Leviathan
Heaved slowly to a halt, hissing, sniffing, snorting
Like a mighty, miffed n' browned-off Trojan bull;
I entered with trepidation sealing myself in — 370
Soon as I was seated, the carriage gathered pace,
Whisking me into muggy darkness undiscovered.

On the flickered carriage wall the artery of this line
Bled from Beja black to a Sea-Green sublime,
Or so it appeared in the light's moth-hovered glow —
To my dumbfounded sights I read some station names
I'd not heard of in all my ramshackle Capital
Days (had they built another City, underground?);
The next stop tantalised: WINSTANLEY COMMON —
Then, LILBURNE ROAD ... I scanned along ... ROBERT
OWEN JUNCTION... 380
SMILLIE CIRCUS ... RUSKIN SQUARE ... MARX'S ARCH ...
PANKHURST GARDEN —

I'd discovered another London off the Sea-Green Line
Where soot-black City and purple Metropolitan fused
Like two honing arteries at the cardio-junction
Of the beating heart of another city accessed through
The slow dark subterfuge of tube —

I alighted to

Discover what alternative Capital waited over-ground
At the summit of the tall, light-spiralling stairwell.

V The Secret City

First thing that struck my pies blinking into sunlit vision,
Settin' me' raspb'rry tart all a-thump and ticker, 390
Me' gormless mouth gargoyle-agog,
N' me' brain a-Colley Cibber,
The cleanness of the pavements, carved from pumice,
Pristine marble terraces towering high immaculate,
Imposing homely monuments, vast statues built to stand
All time and tribulation, lived-in by levelled citizens
Each of equal but individual station; crucial splinters
Of the City-Soul, vital sparks of industry, art, music,
And literature, enriching redistributively,
Furnishing all lives with mortal comforts plenty 400
To inspirit and empower, nurture gifts to grow
From level ground and flower, cultivate the skies
Of animistic light uniting sundered faculties
Of chambers split bicameral in Dark Capital Ages
When Messrs Pecksniff, Chuzzlewit and Tigg expertly filched
Their neighbours' crusts through cold-collated schemes,
Cajoling profits, fattening coffers, not for great works
Of public benefit but to glut in-growing greed
For comfort conched in pin-cushions of consciences —
And, to add insult to mass injury, to afford 410
The likes of them exclusive rights to castigate the unemployed
As idle, the impoverished as spendthrifts, while besides
These turret judges idled, juggling fruits they plucked once ripe,
Polished by sweats of others' subterranean labours
Whom they reimbursed with debts, rent-keep they called 'wages',
The taxable blackmail they termed 'employment' —
Who tailored a making on the backs of ragged benefactors
Bleached on racks 'n' grateful, cowed and black-leg sable —
Save those h'annually striped for wild cat strikes, lambasted for
How they brought the whole bloomin' country to a standstill 420
So more often than not succumbed to bribes — all so
These Business Dons, Capitalist Tsars, grubbing Succubus,
Could sub their gross addictions, indulge in shady vagaries
Of vice couched in rococo in boudoirs' peccadillo,
True leeches on Society but abstracts when the blame

For sudden slumps belched up for their robbed gain
N' pilfered plums: then, the trump-card of their game:
Scapegoat the strokes of those who labour in their name.

But that's all in another time now eyes behold the shine
Of this secret City built on compassion's foundations, 430
Incorruptibly shod: on each clean-tiled face, mounted
On silver slabs, numberless beatified names, tributes
To transit spirits living in tintinnabulating bricks:
Here live the Such-n-suches who mortar bricks with laughter;
Here live the Sundries who share each day making cakes rise
With animated conversations; Here live some children who
Photograph their dreams to inspire their slumbering parents;
Here dwells a family mesmerised by floral fantasies
Wallpapering their days, Acanthus, Larkspur, Aspiritstra;
Bright inscriptions in singing streets — billboards bore luminous 440
Slogans: *"Giving Is Living, Living Is Giving; "The Camel Stalls*
At the Needle's Eye"; "Money Is the Root of All That Withers";
"Prophets, Not Profits"; "True Work Employs Our Hearts and Minds";
"Fill Your Home With What Is Beautiful And Useful"...

I, a startled tourist, now panting breathless in delight
At stumbling on this lost Utopia, overwhelmed by
The intangible gains of imagination's trains
Of shored-up time, as when the sleeper wakes...

...from the clocking, tocking, six'o'clock-choked world
Of rioting whortleberry walls, rankling carpets, 450
Despotic objects, Lilliputian obelisks,
Gauche vases, frilled lampshades, miniatures, inanimate
Paraphernalia clamped as patterned carpet-bags;
The morbid taxidermy of life's stolen moments;
Grisly pastime of gusto-sucked Victorians
(Thick-curtained vice for doily-fogged Rippers,
Or Sickert's impasto Whitechapel set);
Nostalgically embalmed, neurotic
Edwardians' gingering harbingers —
Gloom-browed, mutton-chopped Old Testament Prophets; 460
Orangoutangs in cravats and frockcoats;
Naturalist-rapt, table-tapped Social Darwinists —

All cant, disdain, chicanery, Walrus whiskers, kedgeree,
Flanked by stern-mandibled whalebone wives,
Crushed-velvet aunts, crape-veiled Grand Havishams
Ear-trumpeted beyond the muttered grave
Pickled in dark rooms of jungling rubber-plants
Tetchy with tsetse tinnitus, grotesques
Photographically stuffed for scowling display —
Spoils from a Galapagos of motley drolleries — 470
Puritanically captured; antinomian insects
Startled in alkali, depicted indelibly
In bromide's judgmental amber, thronging
With cased moths and grubs on the groaning mahogany
Sideboard of gothic curiosities,
Mementos of guilty addictions to mangrove
Swamp elliptical, heathen-seething thickets
Of pithed explorers' spoils, Zulu calf-hide shields,
Watussi plumes, Tanzanian dolls, leather-bound
Illicitly thumbed Burtons and Arbuthnots, 480
Collecting entomological sentiments;
Tyrannising light-thirsting minds; stalling
Tall thoughts of scaffolding descendants
Bowed to the worship of mantelpiece-plinths…

…but magically here, in this World Turned Downside-Up
I presently entered, I was butterfly-surprised
By its intangible dimensions, not a rustling trace
Of the dark Capital age I'd unknowingly escaped,
But all those old ideas thought flightless as Dodos
By shadow-folk back there, those old starchy Jingoes, 490
Now flocks of fandango-bounding flamingos:
Everyone on equal ground, no class, no Lords, no Dames,
No brass, no balls, no la-de-das, no dangling chandeliers,
A rolling out of double-barrels, a closing-off of ranks;
No more need for humid Empires' dustbowl colonies
In Darkest lands, to loot ripe fruits, n' more bally bananas,
No more sand campaigns, Sudans and Crimeas,
No soldiers, so no wounded, nor Florence Nightingales
To moth about with lanterns in bloodied farthingales...

What pleased me most, an absence of shops n' 'aggling stalls, 500
Crash of tills, cash-tricks for goods past kosher quota,

No cons on browsing wool-eyed customers, no wheeler-dealers,
No theft, so no need for Bow Street Runners, Sweeny peelers;
Public services publicly run — I'd never seen so many trams!
No more trump of *In the Shadows*' tumpity-tum, now band-stands
Brassed in sunlit upland parks *Out in the Blasting Light!*
To trip the waddling feet of ladies on the duck-tail beat
Of promenades pompomed with pinned-hats and parasols,
Chignon-fastened pillboxes of aigrette floral trimmings,
Scotch Glengarry caps, plateaus, casquettes and ruched tulle, 510
Chaperoned by striped seersucker drakes in Oxbridge boaters;
Out with plodding proms' tiddly-om-pom-pomps and in with
Galloping allegros for all!

Old Mister Clissold
'll short-change himself something chronic: here, a two day
Week, five day weekend — no perfumed, powdered pedigree
To monopolise pulchritudinous hobbies
For beeswax Madame Tussaud hands, while coal-groomed moles
Scrubbed up with oily tallow soap (olfactory stamp
Of their class); caged canaries choking in the damp
Illiterate pits; drones rocking to factory dins; 520
Bow-legged worker bees with rickets, cramped as pit-ponies;
Cloth-eared donkeys doped by carrot-doles n' pipe-dreams
Clogged with jellied-eels, potato peels — lumpen mete
From that jammy-humped Camel of Threadneedle Street —
But every soul at liberty to spend the lion's share
Of their life's hours sculpting their potential in the taper
Of Miriam Sorwill's kaleidoscopic wallpaper;
No private property, every house an open door;
No pickpockets, felons, thieves, as no-one wants for more;
No more famished stomach cramps howling hooperzootics: 530
No needle-eyes magnified through old myopic optics;
No more need for debtors' prisons, workhouses, asylums,
Dank mad-houses clamouring with faradised alarums
Sealed with Caius Cibber's raving Abraham-men —
Only the world of Money had need to build a Bethlem,
There's no cause for madness in harmonious Jerusalem;
No business here for hunks or pawn-broker gain,
Nor any other grubby-fingered legerdemain
No more need for milky hops in smoky rookeries
Of nauseating taverns, nooks of *Ye Old Cheese*; 540
No more blood-rouged fruit-and-veg-head Duchesses of night,

Rate brass flutes with itchy Hounslows touting out of sight;
No more bums-on-seat n' strumpet-strutting music halls'
Tipperary's, *Ta-Ta Leicester Square*'s n' trooping vaudevilles;
No more coffeehouses thronged with politicking tongues,
Bigots of *the Cocoa Tree* and other haunts of Pall Malls' lungs;
No more cloudy brows in rag-partitioned opium dens;
No more poor man's tip-bits: jugged hare and peach melba —
Goodbye galvanic Charlotte Street, ta-ta to Mr Jackin's
Soup buffets and stale crusts and vegetable-peel kitchens; 550
No more evening dreadfuls, *The Gutter Snipe, The Daily Trump*,
To titillate old gouty dad and his nerveless daughters
In the dusty daffs of shaded lamps; no more upstairs-downstairs
Shenanigans of servant-trouncing snobs lording over
Gossip of postprandial pantries, scurrilous sculleries;
No more drab refinement, shapeless fripperies;
Walls of willow or pomegranate, curtains twill and green;
Salons or boudoirs; lavender brilliantine;
Antimacassars; nasal swells and drawls;
No more need for coveting your neighbour's crust or 560
Ego-profiting on others' empty kitties; nevermore,
Untrusting misanthropic twitches of skeletal net-curtains.

An absence of pubs for people punch-drunk
On conversation: *'course you know why they've never*
Got rand to a revolution in the uvver London don'cha'...?
(Apart from the Industrial one). It's tea, that's what it is.
Makes 'em apafetic, complacent-like; summing in the brew;
It's their Spiritual Gin 'see, make no bones abaat it...
— This is it...
They says the h'ancients' come up with it tryin' to distil 570
'eaven' in a drink — but it's Purgat'ry if you adds milk...
— Price of butter mate...
Gin was never so in-si-di-ous as tea is, a propa' manna,
Makes you feel all warm inside, content in your place
Without the need for an educative 'air of the dog next day...
'Avin' said that I miss it meself, 'speshly in the mornins...
— 'Orses for courses cock...
But getting' up to a salmon-sky dawn, no false'un neiver,
Nippers singin' in the streets, whole bleedin' city greetin' you
As one big 'appy fam'ly — none of this flesh 'n' blood lark 580

They string out back there, nah, 'ere we all muck in togeva',
N' ev'ry neighbour's yer China, as like your patent bruvva',
No nippers squealin' with empty bellies, no pover'y...Nah
— Sunny side up...
... I can get by wivout cha...

This secret London: Society of intelligence prised
Patiently by pamphlet-thumbing Fabian firesides,
Symphonised by folkloric composers, dramatised
In Shavian *Pygmalions*, and planted in coal miners'
Torch-haloed heads, now a sharp reality, well-defined 590
As sun, a hovering pit-lamp in the white night sky:
By the time on my watch it was well past nine
At night, yet arbitrary daylight still poured
Yolk on stucco turrets glistening with magic,
An urban Camelot caught in blazing daubs by
Pre-Raphaelite brush; the blossoming symptoms
Of finally flourishing altruism,
Broken out into an epidemic
In rashes of sharing — not rashers of shares —
Blissfully incurable for *the Germ* it spawned from: 600
The palpable bloodline of angels pumped through
The page-turning, caterpillar-spinning ages,
Now bursting out into the cabbage-white light —
See the tumbling flowers, galloping Marigold,
Capillaries of Apple, Harebell and Pimpernel,
Come off on the hands like gossamer colours,
Growing from the walls, weaving and thrusting
Their petals and stems, endorphin-fused tendrils
Intertwining spirits, souls, hearts and minds;
Binding all in a Togetherness brocade; oneness 610
Of purpose; a pan-telepathy of labours;
A prospect of un-forbidden fruits; shimmering
Ideality; poetry tangibly manifest
In this unlikeliest of cities — a pounding Utopia
Of pillar boxes, rainbow-pigeons, fairground laughter,
Where postmen compose poems and poets bring the post;
Correspondence by cross-couplets; and milkman-song
Choruses on levitating bottled-honey floats.

VI Keir Hardie Street

Then — well stone the crows! I scarce believed my pies
As I beheld the striking sign: KEIR HARDIE STREET 620
In pristine ivory lettering on glistening coal black;
For minutes the brilliant white words dazzled me till I felt
I'd topple from the kerb, trip like billeted Whittington
With baggage, tags and famished cat, cash-strapped n' class-scrapped
Only to rise tall and prosper —

A vision I had lit
Before me in piercing mist on this hypnotising street,
Of its gifted namesake, his pit-face rise from Satanic
Collieries, Caledonian obscurities,
Into the light of politics, calloused hand campaigning,
Who strove to lift the people with winging words, help all 630
Prosper, not just kith and kin and his own interests but
Emphatically the whole — humanity *primo franca*,
Descended from the dust and ribs of Common-held Eden
Corrupted by lopsided scales of serpentine greed
Hissing scabrous syllables: *Capitalism*
Spouting from billboards on peeling city walls
Whilst Socialism muttered to itself in draughty halls!

...In Whittington's city, among the Pillar'd Mansions
Of Wren's grand vistas and esplanades,
Another fire catching the wind ignited, 640
Not in gutted Pudding Lane, but farthest Lanarkshire,
Its touch paper smoking in the undernourished clutch
Of a baker's cadaverous delivery boy
Waylaid amid errands by sudden lightning flash
Striking him down, a la Damascus,
A hoi polloi Paul on his way to St. Pancras...

Down the line from Christ the Communist,
'Our Head Leveller', as coined his cousin Baptist
(Though we can trace through Kleisthenes
To Solon's 'Shaking Off of Burdens'), 650
A line of Visionaries, Radicals, Prophets
Strove to oppose the Draconic Rule of Profits,

Chivalrously crying *Redistribution!*
Thomas Beckett itching with idealisms in
His hair-shirt, sandaling beggars' feet; Robin
Goodfellow hooded in Lincoln-green stilling
The bow-hand; Wat Tyler striking Blackheath blows
Against an avatar of tyrants; Thomas More
Scaling castles in the air where star-eyed citizens
Lived according to their needs, as hermitic 660
Crab, the 'Mad' Haberdasher, consecrated
With sacraments of dock-leaf and ditchwater,
A mercury-dipped, wing-footed water-treader
Freed into *being* by shedding his *living*,
Unburdening his dromedary of shop and goods,
The very clothes he wore, to the un-preserving poor
To opt out from the Vanities as an anchorite,
Trip with invisible wings into the violent light
At that same-timed Buckinghamshire where Levellers
Delved ever deep in the scrubland velveteen, 670
Broad flapping hats plumed with Black and Sea Green —
The Diggers pitched a Golden Age at St. George's Hill,
Ploughed Cobham clod with egalitarian till;
Robert Owen's workshop co-ops hammered out a hew
To chop off Class's branches; the Chartist martyrs
Trampled by plumed hooves at Peterloo;
The red-hearted Romantics, courting Napoleonics;
The 'Poetic Upholsterer's class-transcending patterns;
The incandescent canvases of fired Pre-Raphaelites,
Frock-coated revolutionaries of colour politics; 680
Vincent's charcoaled labourers, cloddy pauper daubs
Worshipping potatoes on the blasted Borinage;
Scholarly colliers inspired in spiritless pits;
Marx's pamphlet-sweated 'old clothes-shop of ideas',
Synoptic Social Gospels long-pantomimed in
Galanty-shows of low-born pews and high-brow bowers
Where ever the Rich man shared hymned persiflage
With trembling soap-hands of Fabians;
Where ever the parsimonious Parson
Went hand in hand with the Mammon alms 690
Of the Owner of the glove-grabbed Land:
From this union of penny-pinching piety
Sprung the Chimera we call Charity!

Along the blurring margin of an endless British sunset,
An Empire merging colours to disguise feudal intent —
From *And When Did You Last See Your Father?*
To What Shall We do for the Rent?
Englishness disowns its own apple of radicalism,
Of windfall ideals, for starry-leafed shelter
In the groaning Oak's lengthening shadow. 700
Time again for Commoners' crop-head Opposition
To titled Abusers of Privilege — not
Seen since times of the tailed lobster-pot:
For a sullen and scowling class sitting apart
Is preferable to a besotted and unthinking class
*Dragged hither and thither by unscrupulous guides.**

Turn the other cheek, we may, but only after
We've over-turned the rustling tables and spilt
The stinging metals to the floor, turned stone to bread,
Water into wine, sent camels packing back out through 710
The swelling needle's eye, along with tyrannies,
Titles, honours, property, aristocracy and Kings,
Until the grind and clamour of industry is mute
And we hear Angels singing to the sound of dropping pins.

VII News from Somewhere

The vision's light faltered into pitch-black and shrank,
Then, flickering dimly in the Tartarus dark,
A black hand haloed in a wavering pit-lamp
Scratched Arabesque characters with a darning pin
On the pit-wall's palimpsest, parading
What could be misconstrued as primitive cave etchings, 720
His concentrating hand breathing limb and sinew
Into Sanskrit menageries of shorthand shadow-animals
(The other source for Pitman?) — tortuous script shod,
His grub-white gollywog lips blew the coal-dust away
Like a lady shaking talc to avoid the lampblack blotting —
Not a grind of a lifetime he'd find his hard won way
To the cloistered colossus of matchstick Parliament,
Its gothic fossil-halls, green-leathered misericords,
Downing Street's tempting ebon tiles glistening only
Debates and carbon-paper streets away, 730
Its summoning coal-black face so close, at arm's length
To his Tantalus clutch, but only ever to be
A glimpse, as a bramble's ripest blackberry.

This vision soon returned its sparkled focus, glinting,
A silver plate catching in the sun, whit'ning my sight:
I saw a grimy street in place of that bright, brilliant
One before, to a scraggily built, dowdy-togged young man
Hunched before a glooming bookshop window
Straining his tiny eyes at the tantalising pictures
Spine-spread before him in the open-armed books: 740
James Keir Hardie squinted at the printed fictions
At the turned corner of his scholastic mission —
But he'd learnt to read between the castellated letters,
To untold stories, sins of omission!

Born in a haunted corner of Scotland, of kelpie-
Humped lochs and Pan-piped galloping woods,
Close to Claverhouse's groomed dragoons;
Illegitimate son of a servant-girl from Legbrannock,
Step-sired by an atheist carpenter,

Schooled in obscurity's cramped one-roomed house, 750
Raised on porridge oats and Robbie Burns —
'Lines on Seeing A Wounded Hare'
Fuelled him on compassion's damp-steaming anger —
Fired in the pit of his belly's grumbling brogue,
Conscience-lit by spark of injustice at first hand
As a brow-crowded child, a Little Father Time
Gifted burning vision, he cast off Calvinism,
Its hair-shirt's thorny tag of predestination
For Saved elects, Damned masses — abject castes,
Eschatological parallels to class — 760
Into the mind's abyss, anathema as gallow hills,
And donned the kinder spun Baptist overalls,
Marched with the miners to massed Annbank brass,
Learnt to speak in temperance meetings, teetotal of tongue,
Soap-box for a pulpit, tugged himself up rung by rung,
From blacklisted collier to collared correspondent
For the Airdrie District — editor of *The Miner...*

Then Politics: Member for North-West Ham,
Took his seat in Parliament in red tie and tweeds,
Alternate cap or deerstalker, no frockcoat for he, 770
Braced in proletariat spiritual khakis;
Mrs. Grundy almost fainted when she scanned
*The costume of the new-comer** but for her
Smelling salts — O what a brouhaha!
So offended was she by this chiselled, bearded pauper
Replete in blue serge double-breasted jacket,
Fawn-coloured trousers, striped flannel shirt,
Scarf round his neck in a sailor's knot.

There stood shabbily-clad young Keir
Gifted this insight into his own future, 780
O what a story it promised to be; his deep-
Set quick brown eyes, like sunshine distilled
Through water, squinted rivetingly
To read his yet-to-happen histories,
Fantasies away from grim digs and rivet-fitting,
On the breathless page of posthumous foxing
In the bookshop window of Glasier's ghosting:

Sent down the coal mine when a bit laddie of eight...
Unable to sign his name on the membership pledge
Of the Good Templers... so ashamed he set to work 790
To learn to write... — what lightning he'd write —
The fisherfolk apostles in the New Testament
Would find themselves more at home in the company
Of Keir Hardie than in any other member
Of the House... Emphatically a man of the future...
Yes: for here he was reading far-mapped
Days he had yet to live, a past yet to begin, trapped
As he still was in the milk-skin of infant
Privations, gifted two-way vision as all seers —
The boy started at his clairvoyance of sight 800
As he saw his future foxish face, feral-browed, keen-eyed,
Ear-pricked and whiskered, howling storm-filled speeches,
Thunderously tub-thumped sermons hollered from his pulpit
In Pharisaic Parliament to the bash of gritted fists:
The still small voice of Jesus the Communist
Stole over the earth like a soft refreshing breeze
*Carrying healing wherever it went...**
Then in a stroke he tumbled by the mighty blow
Of pugilist opponents' vocal wrecking-balls;
A drubbing by the jingoes!
An air-snatched gasp 810
Came from the mouth of the ragamuffin stooped
By the bookshop window, flaking loaves in arm,
Smudge of rushing breath on the sunless glass
That started melting before his surprised pies,
Trickling back to grains of hourglass sand
Till it dissolved away, unsealing the books
From their glass palisade; tantalising pages
Long-un-fingered, flailing in the *Daisy* balm
Of the waxing streets, whipping up to blustered
Currents, flexing zephyrs, pugilist gusts 820
Shuffling page on page as if a pack of cards
Little Keir's enraptured eyes reading ever fast
For their hungering need to witness published future,
Not posthumous, precognitive — but the bitten ending
Spluttered out...

...his twilight years witnessed this scene:
Retiring Leader of the Rose (having passed the baton
On to ever keen-eyed Arthur Henderson);
A harassed old white-haired lion of politics, Aslan
Of Socialism, fatally mauled by the mocking
Goblins of the Commons, crawling back into 830
Obscurity's dreary den, amid
Dull mundane thuds of book-packing...

Books marked birth, death and the gristly bit
In-between, for hackneyed centuries;
Life is, was, will be, had always been
One languorous-long shelf bookended end-to-end —
But now the books flew free into the vanishing streets
With a flapping of pigeon-plumed pages, for words
Were always meant as wings to lift Humanity,
Or prolong Its spiritual hesitation — 840
What hope for us without imagination?

Dreams and ideas are still the staple diet
Of the downtrodden, needy, the thoughtful poor,
Who, lacking the clothes of a decent education
Crave the bread of un-judging literatures,
The mind's opium-dens of Gospels and scriptures,
And for some, whether to fall foul or prosper by,
That manipulated, sour-mouthed, opinionated monster,
Politics, Behemoth of Progressive and Modern,
Rung-grasping Grappler of the social climber 850
From Parliamentarians down to Whigs,
The banners of Social Justice fluttered,
Flags of flagrant subterfuge
For factional rung-ups of class-laddering,
Cynically risen on radicalising
Tides of dissent under Commonweal sails
With scamping small print whispering:
'One-upmanship for All; All for One-upmanship,
Behold the Landed fall to Capitalising'.

Only manifestoes inked in sweat of those who've known 860
Injustice at first hand ever meant what they said

And what they said was all they meant, implicit
In letter as scripture, no scrimp-print clause;
Now one such scribe, before his time, witnessed
The darkness-parting truth too starkly lightning-bright
To be inked on paper — the invisibly versed books
Spilled into the streets on wings of onion-skin,
A thousand flocks of vanilla doves tumbling
Throughout the pin-silent Pillar'd Mansions,
Tree-lined vistas, levelled esplanades 870
Of this inimitable City;

Little Keir,
Scruffy, unkempt as a street-scummed urchin,
Knelt on the ground to finger the pages
Of a moss-bound book, apparently blank,
Liberated from the clamping of print —
Something resembling a freak summer breeze
Ruffled the pages like a Japanese fan
Or a lady's rustling taffeta dress;
The tome's only words, a title: *News from Somewhere*,
First published product of a Transparent Classless 880
State, where the People now owned themselves
And the Means to their own Publication.

Up got little Keir, white face no more knitted
With testaments to punished innocents,
His fox-eyes gleaming edified, free
Of resentments of old-world bitterer times;
Now he — and I stood mind-lit on a corner —
Could see quite clearly with illumined pies
The point is to one day catch ourselves up
And spill like free radicals into one whole, 890
So the labours of those cloud-soldiers of old
Will not be in vain; our words never be
Ends in themselves, but means to unbind us,
Wipe credit's slate clean, false debt's palimpsest,
While ledgers go the way of swine in Gadarene —
Meantime, we will heed: to aim for the dream
Is the path to perfection, the dream driven in us
To inspire us in binding a new Social Bible,
Let scaffolding climb to build Lilburne and Blake's

Emerald Jerusalem from sulphurous rubble 900
Of pawnbrokers, pubs and Satanic boutiques,
The tumourous growth of sprawled slums and slagheaps,
As those Other Londoners with their City Turned
Downside Up, off the Sea-Green Line where Bird-
Folk glide off the ground on swan-collar wings
Throwing skyward shadows on dwarfed hoardings —
For there's no need for feet
On KEIR HARDIE STREET.

Notes

Allan Jackdaw (1891-1918) is a fictitious narrator, a motif personifying the struggling, socially conscious, impoverished writer, based loosely on poet John Davidson and novelist Robert Tressell (author of *The Ragged Trousered Philanthropists*).

'Keir Hardie Street' is composed in a style this author terms 'impasto', after the painting technique most typified by Vincent Van Gogh: a thick application of paint, and vigorous brushwork, in order to achieve a tangible effect on canvas. This author's 'impasto' is an attempt to produce a similar effect through poetry, by thickly applying sense-impressions, images, sounds, descriptions, verbs and adjectives, to achieve a similarly tangible impression on the reader.

There is a spirit of pastiche in certain aspects to the style of 'Keir Hardie Street', partly inspired by the balladry of Rudyard Kipling, whose occasional mock-Cockney patois in poems such as 'Tommy Atkins', is mimicked throughout with the frequent dropping of consonants at the beginning of some words and the inappropriate adding of aitches to the beginning of words that start with vowels. But it is John Davidson's social ballad 'Thirty Bob a Week' – some lines and motifs from which are occasionally alluded to – that most intimately inspires much of the idiomatic style and tone of this work. But of course the core inspiration behind the poem is the extraordinary life of James Keir Hardie. My father's grandmother, whom I never knew, was a devout Christian (Baptist) socialist all her life, and, as my father often tells me, would invoke the name of Keir Hardie religiously, as if it were that of a Saint. Indeed, Keir Hardie's life was almost messianic in its moral and practical absolutes; and socialism, in the early 20th century, was considered by many of its followers not to be a doctrine, but a faith, to which one converted rather than merely subscribed: not simply an idea, a political conviction, but an actual way of life.

Alan Morrison

The asterisked quotes are from Mr. Kier Hardie M.P., W. T. Stead (ed.), *Coming Men on Coming Questions* No: VI, (May, 18, 1905); source: *James Keir Hardie — A Biography* (1921, The National Labour Press Ltd.) by William Stewart, with a Preface by J. Ramsay MacDonald.

7 *Colobus*. Of or like a monkey.
25 *Jacked-stalked slatterns*: Allusion to Jack the Ripper preying on prostitutes.
55 *slopshop*. Slang term for clothes-shop or sweat-shop.
84 *camel humps shrank needle-size*: 'It's easier for a camel to pass through the eye of a needle than for a rich man to enter Heaven' (Matthew 19:24).
103 *Boxer*. A member of a turn-of-the-century anti-European Chinese sect.
116 *Mister Kipps*. The eponymous hero of H.G. Wells' story about a draper's apprentice who suddenly comes into money (later adapted into the musical Half a Sixpence).
124 *van-flagging dilly-dallying on the way*. From the Cockney song *My Old Man Said Follow the Van...And don't dilly-dally on the way...*
131 *cartouche*. Egyptian-style inscription of a name in a ring within a scroll.
132 *penny-farthing*. The original bicycle, with one large front wheel and one smaller back wheel.
134 *Pasha*: Egyptian/Turkish address for higher officials.
135 *stovepipe*. The original top-hat, tall, straight and cylindrical, hence name.
144 *Old China*. From 'china plate'/ 'mate' (Cockney rhyming slang).
149 *primogen-h'iture*. Primogeniture: rule that the eldest son inherits first.
154 *Disraeli's Marble Angels*. Disraeli affectionately termed working-class Tories as 'Angels in marble'.
168 *Pillar'd Halls*. 'From my Pillar'd Halls and broad Suburbean Park', John Davidson, 'Thirty Bob a Week' in *Fleet Street Eclogues* (1893).
198 *architraves of Inigo's*. Inigo Jones (1573-1652), neo-classical architect of post-Great Fire London.
masques of blackness. Allusion to The Masque of Blackness,

a 1605 stage production by Inigo Jones and poet Ben Jonson performed for King James I.

210 *Artist after sunstroke, by voices of absent sitters.* Allusion to painter Richard Dadd (1817-1886) whose schizophrenia was initially put down to sunstroke after being abroad; he later committed patricide and was committed to Bedlam.

234 *scamped.* A term used in Robert (Noonan) Tressell's classic social novel *The Ragged Trousered Philanthropists*, meaning 'botched' — a term we might apply to modern cowboys; this stanza is actually about Robert Tressell/his fictional alter ego, Owen, from said novel.

242 *shell-likes.* Slang for 'ears'.

268 *He hurled himself from off a Cornish cliff.* The tragic suicide of poet John Davidson, on whom this stanza is based.

280 *Tommy Anonymous's.* The Tomb of the Unknown Soldier in Westminster Abbey.

296 *dominackers.* From the child's skipping rhyme 'eeny meeny macker racker hi di dominacker...'

288 *Pearly.* The Pearly Kings and Queens of Cockney London, who wore elaborate black outfits decorated with pearl-white buttons.

282 *Fuzzy Wuzzy.* Nickname for the warriors of the Hadendowa tribe in Sudan, because of their dramatic clumps of hair. *Whirligig.* Spinning, revolving toy.

285 *carrara.* A type of marble.

318 *Lilburne.* John Lilburne (1614-1657), leader of the Levellers, social campaigner and pamphleteer of the 1650s. Walwyn. William Walwyn, egalitarian pamphleteer who authored *The Power of Love* (1643) and *A Manifestation* (1649).

319 *Everard and Winstanley.* William Everard and Gerrard Winstanley, leader of the Diggers, an egalitarian group of the 1650s.

323 *light to embers in Buckinghamshire. Light Shining in Buckinghamshire* was the title of a 1648 pamphlet about suffrage, equality and the end of property penned by a group of True Levellers, or Diggers, with whom Winstanley is thought to have been connected with; it is also the title of a 1976 stage play based on the authors of the pamphlet, by Caryl Churchill.

325 *Phossy-jawed.* An old term for decaying, probably cancerous jaw-bone.

336 *Ambushing Oxford Blues slumbered on green benches/ Of old St. Stephens*. Paraphrased from the Labour Party Annual Report, 1906: '...organised labour as a political force is already a menace to the easy-going gentlemen of the old school, who have slumbered for so long on the green benches of St. Stephens...'

339 *by hand and by brain*. From the 1918 Labour Party Constitution: 'To secure for the producers BY HAND AND BY BRAIN the full fruits of their industry....'

340 *Workhouse Crooks' Tory Woolwich gain*. Will Crooks (185-1921), who was raised in a workhouse, rose to Labour's first MP in Woolwich, a former a Tory stronghold, which he won with a large majority in 1903.

344 *Mr. Pease's easy parties*. Edward Pease was a founding Fabian at whose house the Society's first meeting was held.

345 *Mr. Quintus Fabius poured sugared gradualness*. Namesake of the Fabians, socialist intellectuals of the late 1900s; Quintus Fabius Maximus (titled *Cunctator*, meaning 'the delayer') was a Roman general who believed in waiting for the enemy to collapse from within before striking a blow, hence the Fabians' adoption of the name to describe their belief that capitalism would eventually destroy itself; they called this 'the inevitability of gradualness'.

347 *Idle silver singers of fancy cake-stand days*. From William Morris's *The Earthly Paradise*, L'envoi: 'Earth of the earth lies hidden by my clay,/ The idle singer of an empty day!'

349 *glass coffee infusers*. Paraphrased from Keir Hardie's memoir: '...his wife was pouring coffee from a glass infuser ... I had never before seen such a beautiful thing...'

374 *Beja*. Group of Sudanese tribes.

390 *raspb'rry tart*. Raspberry tart: heart (Cockney rhyming slang).

392 Colley Cibber (1671-1757), actor, dramatist, later poet laureate; son of sculptor Caius Cibber.

405 *Messrs Pecksniffe, Chuzzlewit and Tigg*. Mr. Pecksniff, Martin Chuzzlewit Snr. and Montague Tigg, from Charles Dickens' *Martin Chuzzlewit* (1843).

439 *Aspiritstra*. Deliberate misspelling of Aspidistra, to imply an inspirited version: A-spirit-stra.

456-7 *Thick-curtained vice for doily-fogged Rippers, / Or Sickert's impasto Whitechapel set*. Artist Walter Sickert (1860-1942) whom some associate with the unsolved murders of Jack the Ripper; he used the impasto technique.

460 *Mutton-chopped*. Old-fashioned term for large sideburns.

464 *whalebone wives*. Edwardian dresses were fitted with whalebones.

468 *tsetse*. Tsetse flies are from South Africa and are lethal to horses and cattle.

480 *illicitly thumbed ... Burtons and Arbuthnots*. Reference to the *The Kama Sutra of Vatsyayana* (1883), published by Sir Richard Burton and translated in part by Foster Fitzgerald Arbuthnot.

485 *World Turned Downside-Up*. Allusion to the English Civil War song *The World Turned Upside Down* (1643).

505 *In the Shadows*. A popular Edwardian tune.

513 *Old Mister Clissold/ To short-change himself something chronic*. Hero of HG Wells' social novel *The World of William Clissold* (1926). We must assume Allan Jackdaw is seeing into the future here, or is perhaps in an omniscient afterlife, since he died in 1918 and Wells's novel is dated 1926 – hence the precognitive 'To short-change himself...'

524 *Camel of Threadneedle Street*. Allusion to the Biblical proverb: 'It's easier for a camel to pass through the eye of a needle than for a rich man to enter Heaven' (Matthew 19:24).

527 Miriam Sorwill is an anagram of William Morris, meant to imply he has a female alter-ego in this parallel London.

530 *hooperzootics*. Victorian slang for stomach trouble.

534 *Caius Cibber's raving Abraham-men*. Reference to Caius Gabriel Cibber (1630-1700) who sculpted two giant statues depicting dementia and madness, Raving and Melancholy Madness that lorded over the entrance to Bedlam, known then as Bethlem (after Bethlehem); 'Abraham-men' was a nickname for discharged inmates of Bedlam who begged on the streets.

535 *Bethlem*. Bedlam; originally called Bethlehem and then abbreviated to Bethlem.

542 *Rate brass flutes*. Cockney rhyming slang for prostitutes. *Hounslows*. Cockney rhyming slang for teeth, from Hounslow Heath.

589 *Shavian*. Of or relating to George Bernard Shaw. *Pygmalions*. Shaw's class satire *Pygmalion*, which was later

adapted into the popular musical *My Fair Lady*.

600 *The Germ* was a one-off pamphlet by the Pre-Raphaelites.

604-5 Titles of William Morris wallpaper designs.

649 Kleisthenes (600-527 BC): first democratic leader of Athens.

650 *Solon's 'Shaking Off of Burdens'*. Solon (638-559 BC): Athenian lawgiver and archon who set the foundations for democracy ('rule of the people' from 'demos': people). He freed all slaves from their debts, a policy called *seisactheia* ('a shaking off of burdens').

652 *Draconic*. Draco (7th c. BC): archon of Athens who prescribed the penalty of death for almost every offence, known as the Draconic code; hence the word draconian, meaning harsh, cruel.

656-7 *stilling/ The bow-hand*. '...still the bow-hand of fair justice' (Solon the lawgiver of Athens).

661 *Crab, the 'Mad' Haberdasher*. Roger Crab was a puritan haberdasher who gave all he owned to the poor and retired to live as a hermit in complete austerity so as to, he believed, perfect himself like the angels. Some think him the inspiration behind Lewis Carroll's Mad Hatter.

671 *Black and Sea Green*. The Levellers, who wore black and sea-green feathers in their hats.

678 *'Poetic Upholsterer'*. Nickname for socialist designer and writer William Morris.

686 *Galanty-shows*. A shadow pantomime showed through a screen.

696 *And When Did You Last See Your Father?*. A Victorian painting depicting a son of a Royalist being quizzed by Parliamentarians, by WF Yeames.

697 *What Shall We do for the Rent?*. A painting by Walter Sickert.

723 *Pitman?* 'Pitman' shorthand — Keir Hardie, an autodidact, taught himself to read and write and to write shorthand when working as pit-boy.

725 *lampblack*. Pigment made from soot which used to be used for ink.

745 *kelpie*. Malevolent water spirit in shape of horse; Scottish name for Lochness Monster.

763 *Annbank brass*. The young Keir Hardie joined a Union march at Annbank accompanied by a brass band.

771 *Braced in proletariat spiritual khakis*. Allusion to Hardie's

entry into Parliament in 1900's so-called Khaki Election.

782-3 *eyes, like sunshine distilled/ Through water*. Paraphrased from "deep-set eyes like sunshine distilled, as we see it through the waters of a pool in the brown earth", *The Women's Dreadnought*, Sylvia Pankhurst.

787 *Glasier's ghosting*. Bruce Glasier was a close political associate and friend of Hardie, who had begun assembling material for his biography of Hardie shortly before he died; William Stewart eventually penned and published in 1921.

828 *Aslan*. The Messianic lion from CS Lewis's Narnia books.

879 *News from Somewhere*. The title of William Morris's socialist utopian novel *News from Nowhere* (1891).

895 *Gadarene*. The swine of Gadarene who were possessed by the demon who proclaimed 'My name is Legion', New Testament.

Widdershins Edwardiana?

after J.B. Priestley's *The Edwardians*

The nostalgia-struck historian, sickened in spirit by the chains of his age, the lack of momentum, of radical vision, at the turn of another century's page, trembles with grief at the blankness ahead; the guttering pales his mind to ghost margins – second-hand pasts shape him, memories read…those new-fangled Edwardians. He remembers through other peoples' memories that seem more real to him than the anodyne dream of his own mundane times. He remembers them remembering...

Oliver Onions' spine-tingling *Widdershins*| Band-stands balking *In the Shadows* in the silences between the golden voice of Plunket Greene| Sharp's folkloric bowdlerizing| Galloping Grainger, the jogging pianist, Apollo'd by osmosis of a mother imbibing a Greek God through her pregnant eyes| Down Ampney Ralph cantering *Toward the Unknown Region*| Orbiting Holst| D-D-Delius| Elgar's brassy pomp – a stately paradise away from Kipps's squalid circumstance in slurries of the draperies; *Gerontions* from dry-rot slums of Spitalfields and Whitechapel's damp stacking garrets, punctuated by backyards' mackeracker magpie girls|

|*Remembers them remembering*|

Strang's sharp portraits| Gore's sceptred moments, honeyed in ochre| Sickert's gritty variations of the striking everyday, painting the Ripper at work on Dat Annie, or just some soul worsted with worry at paying the rent| Brake Baldwin's cloudy trees| Uproarious café nonsense|

Hen-pecked Crippen and Ethel Le Neve vanished, then revealed to Liverpool via wireless, the new marvel the felon waxed over, now his nemesis: a baiting by airwaves| 'Peter the Painter' trapped by a brush|

Campbell-Bannerman on course to the top of Parliament,

Liberals bolstered in votes since the swing of Khakis| Asquith howled down in the Commons: *Divide! 'Vide! 'Vide!* to scourge of stamp-licking| The mercurial man from the valleys – radical, or a lackey to capitalists? (Another unanswerable Fabian quandary)|

No time for sleepy compromisers say old 'Diehards' – any drowsy agitator might try for a seat| Lock out of the Boilermakers' Society| Mothers clamouring their kids' empty plates| Apron-string strikes, stevedores, temper-trying summer of '11| A million miners for a minimum wage – a place in 'Cole and Postgate'| Tillet on Tower Hill| Jim Larkin's 'blacking of goods' – co-operative societies| Last 'class conscious' working class – sharpening of cutlass call to arms couldn't compete with a trumpet blast| clarions fomented from the song of sweating labour|

Burning furniture, stoning the Commons, flaming rags in pillar boxes| Suffragettes: misandersists? Not Mrs Despard or Madam Pankhurst| 'Black Friday'| The Pethick-Lawrences withdraw, fly in the face of Almroth Wright's 'a passive appendage to man'| McKenna's Cat and Mouse Act – while lamps gossip in moorland cottages| Martyrdom at galloping Epsom, enough to spill elevenses: Society's *Titanic*| Hubristic folly of men – all just to beat the *Cunardes*|

|*Not forgetting*|

The wonderful Grock!| Vesta Tilley, male impersonator| Abounding tabloids out of Harmsworth's way – but for penny evening dreadfuls – *The Globe* and *Pall Mall Gazette*| Shakespeare a la décor – change from Beerbolm Tree's literal rabbits and gambolling leverets| Round robins of protest| Music hall radicals and Vaudeville| Dear old dad and his daughters under a drawing room's daffodowndilly lamps| Escape from rapier tushery| Verdenne-Barker seasons| Burlesque music hall bacchanalia| St John Hawkin's bowing out for tissues of neurasthenia| Granville's *Waste* promptly banned by Lord Chamberlain's department| Black Ascot| Orage's *New Age*| A pewter-eyed philatelist King Orage's *New Age*|

He remembers all this, though he wasn't there, he sees these things, these needling details more clearly than the dull uniformities of his life and times; daily realities blur, trip invisibly out of spectacled, well-travelled sights. Time travellers needn't get out of their chairs: infinities bristle on the time-ravelled page. No need to engage in a foregone age for a tangible bygone bonanza of facts, passions, achievements, long-engrained acts, costumes and characters, players and mountebanks. No need to look up from the crawling words of the book. The present, the future, are shadows un-cast – can only come to life once they are in the past...

Clocking-in for the Witching Hour

I Setting Off

It's half-past half-past nine'o'clock
so hickery-dickery-dock
tired eyes accuse the clock
as if the mantelpiece were a dock
and the ornaments that clutter it, a jury...

How many ticks to a tock?

As many as holes in this sock,
this tired nylon catch fished out
from the rummaged-in rummaged-out drawer,
then flung back…

...no pairs left, just odd socks,
only this overworked underpaid pair left
wrung out like old rocks...

...two sons left home, no mementos, no
sideboards crammed with beaming photos, no
marriages, no confetti ever after, no
wedding shots, no patters of tiny feet — not yet —
just long-exhausted memories,
postcards haunting from a long-armed past,
abandoned bedrooms, cast-off belongings,
damp paperbacks, lampshade-less light-bulbs,
cobwebbed beams, stopped clocks…

…sunless curtains crumpled on the rail
like old dowdy clothes long grown-out of,
all flown-the-nest fusty, dust and fade,
corpse-still childhood idols — once
looked-to for guidance, now shunned like parents —
peeling off panda-eyed stares from the walls'
dreaming narratives of papunya sockprints...

...peels his sock off, pats on some talcum,
puts his powdered foot back in its worsted working skin,
a bit of spit to polish his scuffed boots, blacking
spittle, black-polish boot-brush in a rush, always in
a rush against the clock, in tick-tock time,
every nerve, muscle and reflex primed
and disciplined as in his service days...

...no, not the soul-lifting service
of Curry Mallet's Somerset stone,
gravely organ-groaning holy-stone,
free to breathe in altar-boy gowns,
ivory white hands clasping the cross,
infant heart beating time to God's
as tumbled headstones dozed outside
in the slumbered hushaby churchyard's
headstones and bramble-misericords...

...chin up, chest out, stomach in, shoulders back,
thumbs in line with well-pressed seams of trousers...

Medieval Cathedral organ grind,
tremulous, still shivers his spine...

...deep-etched, tired-etched, deep-engrained seams
stitch the creases of his skin together, form
the troubled story of his physiognomy, storm
the haggard ramparts of his bags, map his face
with deep depressions, cartographic features,
traces of tight-skinned third-degree scars
from childhood's ignited dressing-gown
combusted by scorched coal growling from
the grate: consumed, morphined, mummified,
lifted to his only taste of true peace of mind
and overwhelming numbness of body...

...shown the light a glowing age ago, embalmed
in lambasting flame which licked his skin
with pinch of sulphur — vividly glimpsed
weightless peace chrysalis-hatching,

tasted a premature ambrosia,
bottleless and bodiless — jolted by imps
dancing on the walls, then the slow drift
back to pale corporeality
pumped back into him with morphine...

condemned to shaky nerves all his life

…to thump down from inexpressible bliss
to duty's leadenness … last-minute tug
of cig… jagged crosswords scored from scissor-
snip, inspects his satchel packed by his
long-suffering suffering wife…

…who once had light in her chestnut eyes,
sun in her tousling hair, before
she learnt to abide the shadows, choke off
her laugh in the unnoticed shade…once had
a spark of defiance about her, now
hibernating, though not forever: you
can never fetch back the tether entire,
but she'd regain her wedding ring
ritually after each annual pawning...

...shambling off with a boot-spit kiss
on the cheek of his drawn bride for life,
he heaves into night to chinking car-keys,
starts the engine, pulls the clutch,
snails his car away till daylight…

...khaki and Royal Marine blue
stole his holy youth…

Has his family tree in mind, flashes
of fond memories as he indicates,
bag filled with clingfilmed sandwiches,
cut-out cryptics from *The Independent*
(*ironed of broadsheet creases*)
to keep his intellect ticking over,
a tattered account of *The Mutiny on*

the Bounty and a well-thumbed library issue
of *The Ragged Trousered Philanthropists...*
stamped beyond return…

To most it's just another slumping night,
to him, one more score on the stark calendar
of the whitewashed walls of his mind,
while he serves out his time…

II Clocking-On

Pulling up to the pant and splutter of rusted
exhaust, he berths his clapped-out burgundy
quixotic Maxi, exhausted already...

sixty years has been a long shift…

... reflections form in the dark windscreen:
his rookish hook-nosed father back at Rock
telling him to pull his socks up, stop
being a throwback doom-and-glooming
Morbid Morrison, as his grandfather before him;

that whisky-whiskered Scotsman

jolting his 'guts-ache' music to scrape
of rutting stylus scratching rustic fantasias

thumping imps down in the dumps

of vinyl Greensleeved valleys, England's
windmilling vaughanwilliams-green,
Seventeen Come Sunday, O Bonny Boy,
Holst's bright-striding Jupiter,
Walton's clarion Crookback score —
tunes that lifted the sword of the soul, or
plunged the mood down into Hardy's dales

aural sanctuary for a natural romantic

of fate, frumenty mistakes, defeat…
tales haunting him through life with cloth feet…
to making amends and tethers' ends' meet…

and tethers' ends ends' meet…

Ten-hundred hrs pm. Time for treading
guard-dog grounds, scraping pay by losing

power, for eight owl-hours clock-watching
and clocking-in for the witching-hour…

They call him Al, Drew, Fred, amalgams
of what they called him yonks ago
at Eastney barracks, 4.2 Commando,
among other nicknames — Jug-Ears or
The Japanese Executioner
when smart as a drill-stick on parade
sharp and bright as a bayonet-blade,
Corporal's stripes, chin-strapped, slash-peaked,
chinky-eyed — they called him Fred…

Roger, Charlie, Ginger Higgins,
Terry Catteral, Tom Crabbe,
Baby-faced Rigdon, Signaller,
Per Mare Per Terram, telegraph wires,
yomping, ciggies, black peat fires…

...gone round in circles like a paradox
(or the mismatching of two odd socks),
back to that botched beginning, barracked
back at the start — he's back in the ranks —

About Turn!
Stand at EASE!

A trembling boy groomed for the clergy
prone to morbid love of the holy,
devout as larks at rising early
pushed in barrack-rooms too soon
lacking the confidence for officer's groom…
pulled himself up through the ranks
of sea-green berets to Corporal's stripes,
from the Globe & Laurel cap-badge to
a Security firm's pale imitation
(*no more a Civil Service SHO*) —
never reached his rightful station …

unjustly feels he's shamed his past:
silver cake-stands, chinking china,
grandmother in stiff-necked dress,
stern sparrowhawk-faced father...

...stations, class, belonging somewhere
suited to his sensitivities: still
to this day, his mushrooming obsession...

III Back in the Mess

Back to barrack-room lavatory banter,
tits and holes and filling holes
(*and what else fits those holes…*)
pensioned-off ex-Bootnecks and Navvies,
pop-bellied, cork-eyed, sold-out of uniformed
thoughts and opinions, fuggy with sighs,
Closed Shop signs in their square eyes;
Benson & Hedges hedging smelling-men
spat in masturbating line,
masticating on tabloid cud...

> *— What you reading this time Al?*
> *Why don't you ever watch TV?*
> *— Because it's just an Idiot's Lantern, thinks he…*
> *— Come on you bookbrow boffin, crack*
> *a can and watch this video nasty...*
>
> *Look but never see:*
> *all you'll find is yourself looking back at me.*
>
> *Blinkered Little Englanders,*
> *tabloid-boggled, fry-up, tits-and-bum men;*
> *TV, satellite-dish, mobile-phones-for-bones men;*
> *hatchback, dick-scratch, scrotum-focused pig-men;*
> *libido-gone, fumbling with pillow-thigh wives men;*
> *chain-smoking, choking, beer-swilling balding men;*
> *thick-fingered, lung-cindered ex-service men…*

This is no place for a thinking man
moved on so far since service days
in his insights (not his pays…),
who's struggled on, survived life's slog,
albeit chipped, half-broken, bruised
by being pushed in the deep end of sweat
and testosterone at green seventeen,
when he lost his innocence to messes' smut,
cigarettes, and shoulder-jolts of rifle-butts…

Visceral vicissitudes: boyish with bumfluff
at virginal seventeen, sensitive, silken-
skinned as a girl, innocent, violated
in valance-carved dark that curved him
in seamy minds of libation-jerking
squaddies in midnight mess – discharged
ashore, hair trimmed, skin brushed by AWOL
hands of the 'best barber in Limassol'

This social chameleon forced to blend in
his nuanced manners, affectations, even speech —
to bruise-blue diction; trying to fit in
with working-class habits as his own class
won't let him back in. (He's a *skidder* as
Sociologists would call him and
the ladder's rungs have fallen in…

FALL IN!).

This ever-recurring repetition
is his idea of Hell, or thereabouts —
surely Purgatory's too vague a thing
to inflict such suffering
a second time round…?

IV First Watch

Bored, over-tired, fuzzy thoughts grow
hypnogogic in the dim torch-glow —

Halt! Who goes there? Friend or Foe?

Not someone — hopefully a ghost?

Come out of the shadows you Holy Ghost!

A headless drummer returns to haunt him:
its footsteps echoed to his sentry in
abandoned glooms of disused barracks,
the phantom beat of hard-shoed feet
drumming down the corridor
tapping on the concrete floor...

like Blind Pew's perspicacious stick
probing about at the Admiral Benbow

...ghost footfall, phantasm-feet,
bent on haunting to regimented beat...

Worst thing he can imagine
comes close, through fatigue, to haunting him
as he lights his last squashed Superking:
that after his mortal demobbing
he'd be sentenced to live his whole life again...

start from stuck-in-a-rut-stylus-scratch

...or worse: sent back to serve time haunting
the places and faces, traumas and mistakes,
ordeals, doubts, fears and empty plates...

wishes for clean slates

...sentenced to serve out his Purgatory

as a misbilleted, ill-suited sentry,
doubt-stricken shade, ill-fitted soul
forever on the existential dole...

out on a limb in limbo

...until he solves its shibboleth…
...sent down to haunt his mortal steps

Is there suitable employment after death?

on the same well-trodden, worn-out path,
patroller of the afterlife...

clocking-in for clocking-out

...guarding his own phantasmagorical
prison — an eternally sedentary sentry…

He's always been humble, vulnerable,
a novice to any ounce of power —
to keep his home, his sons and wife
he's clocking-in for the witching-hour…

forced to plod on till his pension comes through
at sixty-five…now it's ten forty-two.

V Back on Gate

Watchstrap breaks, fag-hand shakes,
shudder shoots through him as if someone sometime
before or since stalks his unmarked grave…

the self-deprecating
opt for cremating

...tapping patters of spitting rain
beat tympanum-drumming fingers on
his cap's shiny rain-beaded peak.
He's too silent to speak.
He sucks on a humbug to the knock of his teeth.

If he were a Scrooge then maybe tonight
old ghosts might grant him kind insights,
but he's more a Bob Cratchit, a classless clerk,
a Reginald Perrin of Suburbiton,

skin clung by damp city air, pinstriped
sleeves heaving with commuter fumes
(*and ashtray sprays of Undergrounds*)
sighs long as the Northern Line
partition-faced, umbrella, brief-case...

many times he's left his clothes
on the pebbly beach
of his shingling mind
like Perrin, Stonehouse, Troy

...high-blood pressure, over-stressed, depressed,
sick to the pits with standing-room-only
odours of politely broken-out sweats,
reeking of rail-fumes, sucking on Valiums
in broadsheet-folding balancing acts…

This plain man with his gingery
old soldier's tache, has spent his life

soldiering through thorny scrub
of obstacles, the wearing rub
of slow-eroding worth, bearing
burdens heaped on him in debts —
he's blamed himself enough and yet
he'll blame himself more time in future
forgetting the arbitrary cards
he was dealt weren't his for dealing —
conceals his pain behind a vulnerable grin…

The honest, trusting and virtuous
are seldom addressed by any kind hand
of fate, Guardian Angel, or god
up in its busy office...
the good go unguided…

Nicotine patches, peppermints,
Fisherman's Friends and Valiums:
prescriptions helping him fend off
high blood pressure, smoker's cough,
nerves and dark depressions ringed
round his baggy shadowed eyes;
faint traces of tiredness fate inflicts
through ceaseless night time shifts…
...his crinkled brow lifts with yawns,
life-pummelled face stretches, extends,
bloodshot eyes blearily focus...

(A young Marine said to him
out on the gate one night,
he reminded him of someone he'd never
known but would have liked to have
— someone out of another time,
interesting, reassuring, comforting
like a shy, reclining old armchair or
a true gentleman with a turn-of-the-
century face defying extinction…)

...it's an interesting face, patterned with age
and faded third-degree scars...

> *...scars that mark his upper arms*
> *pumiced with a glaze of age*
> *and a gradual marbling,*
> *abraded to a glassy map*
> *of scoured contours, nerves eroded,*
> *flared at troubles' plastering,*
> *no bandages for dressing...*

...rumpled forehead (a cattle-grid, or
corrugated iron), disturbed, undulated
by worry's dunes, smooth-warped dunes
like Arabian sands where he'd once supped
with burping Berbers and Bedouin,
awed at Tuaregs' shimmering

inked mirages, drolly bobbing
on dromedaries under burdens
of damask-robed loads, camels groaning
like grumpy humped old men...had his
white Berkshire skin embellished by
pounding Arab sun, first tanned
by its naked un-abating blaze
to the goldening bronze of sailing days...

...Globe & Laurelled cork helmed deck,
gangway whistles, gloved salutes,
boundless skies of hussar blue...

I see his tanned, scarred, shaky hands
drumming his knife and fork on the plate,
despite his rhythm, couldn't be a drummer
for they played bugles too and his teeth
stuck out too much...now he tooth-picks
many faded yellow years later
aft a hearty memory-meal
of Mobile Mushrooms long ago —

now landlocked, anchored at the berth
stagnant shallows, beached self-worth…

…sat on his marching knees
to 'A Life On The Ocean Waves'
he grins as salty sentiment staves
streams like Pacific seas;
cigarette smoke tousles and sails
out from his drumming hands;
whistling teeth biting blunt nails —
cymbal clash of the old Massed Bands
hisses to halt. *Steady*
on the deck of a landlocked lounge he
sways side to side as if still at sea…

Martyr for sake of sentiments,
'a romantic' in his own phrase;
a grammar lad transplanted from
his quaking heart's Berkshire
to Somerset's steep soul...

his is a special type of sensitivity,
to cry so quickly, so easily...

...Strong-souled: match for any Mister Scratch
aficionado — like meddling Tom Crabbe
interrupted amidst a sandstorm attempt
to summon Satan in his tent…
the ironic sight of inoffensive Fred
embodied his apostate disappointment…
…now Crabbe's anathema is stranded far
from Saharan dunes and desert seas…

Now just a pitch-black, boot-polish, bitter,
pitter-patter, splitter-splatter, spit-and-polish sky
spitting down on him outside in dark
unaccommodating countryside…
…no welcome in wild windswept Cornwall
for the up-rooted easterner, townie, limey,
only bleakness and threatening winter…

Devon's no better: crumbled stubborn hills
show no sense of duty to their stranded
inhabitants, burgesses, or urban refugees…
...nothing but ancient darkness, uneven green,
moody moor, jutting tor, brooding inspirations…

...deep bleak reassuring coffin-black dark,
deep dark dug-up doom-and-moody glooms…

...morbid childhood glooms in cosy,
cloying, cidery rooms
on hushed Sunday afternoons,
slumberous tock of grandfather clock
as thundery moods moved over him
interminably trembling,
no rhyme or reason, maundering
in a static hamlet small-holding
at craggy rag-tag Rock in
deepest cheddar-reddest Somerset,
near flat Sedgemoor, the Blackdown Hills,
his stifled spirit lifted times
by Jupiter's pageanting trills…

...raised at Rock, stark jagged heights,
sweeping heath-fields under prows
of brooding tor —rhapsodic Holst-
scored ghost-galloped Somerset
land of eternal early evening:
crags gleaming like crockery
at scrubbed and scoured sunset...

...knights in shining armour, grails,
black-and-white plated battlefields,
chivalry, courtly love, pedestals…

...someone, somewhere, sometime, somehow
summoning him from a honeysuckled glade,
roses ravelled in her Pre-Raphaelite hair,
always called Helen, waiting there…

...*idyllic* Shropshire Lad, Sky West and Crooked,
To Serve Them All My Days *gowned days,*
larks among un-travelled ways,
first kisses amidst the hay-stacks,

scrumpy straight from the apple-barrel,
cycling to school down bookish lanes,
Captain Valiants, Allan Quartermains,
Kipling, Kipps, Skip the crippled
schoolmaster's wheelchair-bound genius,
a highfalutin Fagin grooming his boys
for scholastic pickpocketing — school chums,
Mickey Probert, doomed Jiggs Dunne
opting out in chains down a Plymouth hovel
dugout in a moment one gloom too long
of adolescent darkness...

...from boyhood Somersetting dreams
to this bleak Cornish lack of means,
from bucolic Rock to drab Trematon's
forgotten cottage, its frowning face
of misanthropic stone, lop-sided roof,
crumbling out-house, ramble-garden
clambering for space over a concrete,
chronic, ironic 'Morrison' shelter,
rubble-filled grotto monument
to bygone buzzing bomber drones...

Cornwall or Andover — so he chose,
through the nose, his best friend's offer
of a renovated country cottage
in a hamlet of tremoring name...

Trematon Cottage was once two tenements —
sundered and thunderstruck into one
in later days — barely a beam between them;
and the corpulent coffin of an old shrew who'd
been lifeburied in one side, obese
as a popbelly sow, had to be pulleyed through
the dark-creaked dry-rotted window

sunken in the shrunken cottage grotto-
walls of damp-kneaded, swollen dough...

...a botched picture-postcard country escape
turned scraping reclusion, he wound up ruined,
in debt, unemployed, then bowed down to
the soul-destroying scourge of 'the
quick handover'...
...about now, on time,
his long-suffering tuffeting wife —
once an optimistic life-loving girl
groomed for treading the boards —
careworn, grandchild-longing,
broody for babes long grown up, mousily
checks the meter, turning the key
till it clicks and re-ticks, resuscitates
and thaws the freezing cottage through
with its ration of electricity;
it's haunted, their house, so some used to say
by those living in its unvisited day...

...two mongrel dogs, loyal, misanthropic,
used to be and belong here, part of the place,
hounding out rogue scents outside over
the overgrown, shambling grass, barking
at any slight sound, creak of the cackling
gate's witching hinges, vigilantly guarding
on a paint-peeling blistered window-ledge:
Jacobean-maned Max, *the little man*
in black velvet, rapscallion, and Buster
the foxy fellow, rufous-furred, farouche —
both *couchant guardant* (their Master would say
in bleared contentment's heraldic humour
tripping his mind's lighter cartouche)...

...A light balm in a late makeshift Cornish
summer all ramshackle, cack-handed
piskie-tinkling light; a wheezing,
chest-crackling old crofter's ghost,
lambchopped and slumber-eyed,
wiping the crinkled sweatbeads from

his pastee-platted brow, callused
of tan as a gnarled goaty oak... Old Janner
the knock-kneed yokel Tamaritan farmer
tolerates us; stamps his oat-breath on
the oddly chilled air, hooks sun-bitten hand
on a nail on the low-lying, brindled beams
of the partly living room... 'They're not
from around 'ere', his after-trace
articulates from a moth-hatched throat,
'Townies I reckons, but they not all bad,
'n' I'm tired o'hauntin' barren barns.
Sure as the weathercock spins, I can
do with they foreigners' comp'ny...'

...the dogs rise, scamper to the waxy
window-ledge all scratch, scrape, sniff,
sneeze, snort and whimper, crabbily
gabbling half-awake barks for sudden
whistle-chill limbering in to interrupt
their rug-begrudged sleep. With colourblind
portals to ever-present minds
they discern the tacit tones of a spirit
visitor, his contours, tactile character,
loping gait o' wood-style broke, anachro-
-nistic scent of faded autumn fields,
ruminated cow-cud tobacco, intermittent
manifest face of cracked past and waiting,
craning over their startled tails. They're
dumb for want of rotating tongues to be
our translators — flabbergasted in the laps
of ghost-blind gods — our bicameral
sense needle futilely to describe
our invisible guest on the tracing paper
of our starved spirit-itch to pin
the afterlife to a pyrrhic certainty,
(for why bash and scrape down here if
an after-life's only a bolt of breath away?).
Strain our crude-discerning irises we might,
it'll not light our materially misted sight,
can't see beyond the grain, the texture of things,

and this frustrates us into half-baked faiths,
agnostic doubts, thanatos, apostasy,
or the slow-staining damp-patch of atheism
(dogs, alone, are devout believers)...

...the brother dogs, while they lived,
straggly-maned, straddled-legged, wild,
starved of decent exercise...

cooped-up for fifteen restricted chickens-
in-a-wire-run years in scruffy confines
of a ramshackle garden's fenced enclosure
for gnarled-faced, barrel-girthed farmers
daubing the hamlet fields with low-
sweeping clouds of puffed sheep

...kept their doting mother company
whilst their Master suffered nightly
shifts, with boundless, unconditional
love; they comforted, protected,
their snoring mangled weight keeping
her safe and sound in the warm damp bed
till morning light yawned through the curtains
to announce her husband coughing home...

...now in the unlimited fields of hereafter
her husband likes to think they roam...

The mongrels they coined Sussex Hounds,
an inimitable breed, their only
sentient friends since they moved down
with their two rootless sons to this
suspicious-staring Cornishness,
out in the shipwrecked sticks,
where town-hewn innocents were trapped
by country-carved corruptions...

Piskies never grant a wish
so turn your cheek from the Cornish kiss
oh that fickle Judas kiss
the Judas kiss of the Cornish

VI Out of Clock-Time

…clocking-out for half-an-hour's grace,
frozen-boned fag-break, pull of face,
bite of stale sandwich, sip of stewed tea
in hand-thawing mug of memory…
Sixty now but still not free,
no more than at recruited seventeen,
smartened up for first inspection
on the parade-ground at grey Eastney…

from the grey stone of Eastney
to the red brick of Bickleigh

You can keep your Kipling and his 'If',
there is no If about it;
put away your *Plain Tales From The Hills*
for the plainer truth of things,
more the hard tacks of *Barrack Room Ballads*

Baa! Baa! Barracks

for one of life's 'Gentleman Rankers',
leave the dampstained Allan Quartermain
to its dusty buckling shelf,
for Rider Haggard's straggled-haired
hero's shadow-worshipper
is now in Security, insecure,
un-pensioned, discarded, obscured as Jude
(*but conscious of his Little ticking son*)
a self-abasing disinherited Jim...

blames himself for not withstanding
his own biding Gentleman Brown
waiting for him to drown

...the force of a gale's implacable hands
pushing him into jumping

slow circumnavigation of an innocent
storm-tossed conscience
racked by thoughts of self-desertion...

overboard into tampering waves
of Neptune's cryptic captaincy
crossing the line through pilgrimage...

shellback, pollywog, give a god a throne,
tar-black, gollywog, he came rolling home

...of unmerited punishment, outcast
atonement, and last-ditched gesture, left
to right, then Davy-down with anchor,
plunging into the figment of failure...

...failure bites at its own fingernails;
only fate's interpretation fails...

The Defendant finds himself guilty
of his own powerless misfortunes
and hereby sentences himself to see
himself as a Failure...

...to be haunted by long-sold ghosts
of old pawn-brokered heirlooms...

...he winds up here again...
(*tock, tock, tock, tock...*)
at an interminable Twelve-Ten —
well into the witching-hour...

'O to be a bed'
Morpheus once said

Thoughts trace back his family tree
into fathoms of ancestral memory
to keep his frustrated intellect ticking
into itinerant hours like the noiseless tripping
of the heart, whose necessary valve-like motion...

thumping, pumping, pumping

...forms a thought that makes him ill...

thump, thump, pump, pump, pump

...to think our lives, thoughts, emotions,
feelings, souls, experiences
depend upon this butterfly in the chest,
this fluttering thumperty-thump, to exist
until it decides to desist...

...Shoosmith, Parker, Ogle, Asgill...
William Charles Baronet disinherited
his nameforsaken son for stooping
in love and status — if he hadn't then
his brow-depressed descendant, this
damp-jumpered huddled muddled man
might be a Baronet-but-one
of Asgill House on the rolling banks
of Richmond's scrolling Thames...

house of his ancestor, Lord Mayor of London
for whom that ormolu coach was forged;
his family's Dick Whittington
to Tumbledown Dick down the line...

...further sip of genealogical tea...
further still into mists of heredity
to mysterious Mr. Asgill MP...

... a cryptic ancestor if ever he traced one,
a *Who's Who/Great Irish Eccentrics* entry
back in the musty 12:17-th century:
John Asgill, Honourable Member for Bramber
(*scatty eschatological Mad Hatter*
like Roger Crab's berried haberdasher),
a quizzical insect trapped in amber,
antinomian-cum-impuritan,
legalistic libertine interpreting the

Bible with his lawyer's eye literally,
pioneered his eponymous theosophy
on Man's ability, by legal right,
to translate to the afterlife
before His natural time;

An Argument proving, That according to
the Covenant of Eternal Life revealed
in the Scriptures, Man may be
Translated from hence into that
Eternal Life, &c.

Translation he called this circuitous clause,
believing that Man did not have to die...

did not have to die…

...deep, discontented, gravelly sigh…
...breathes out tousling clouds of smoke…
Clouds! Translated Asgill claimed
could ceremoniously transport those
through literal Translation…

Altho'
the Human Nature of CHRIST Himself
could not be translated till he had passed
through Death…

....for Christ died for our sins
so we might live forever…
(*beyond the end of the tether…*)
...no need for us to resurrect:
we can *translate* to the elect...

When Asgill's pamphleteering lungs
pumped their grampus-spuming last
mid-proselytising another clause,
they posthumously honoured him
'*Translated* Asgill' — a man of dreams
but metaphysically limited means,
or so it seems, no more…

Sometimes in hours of probing doubt,
mental darkness, lack of faith
and Gethsemanite state of mind,
tear-stained, slurred with lager,
he wished he too could opt for his
old translated ancestor's
get-out-clause, crawl on a cloud
and spirit off to bliss and tea-things
of an inherited heirloomed Heaven...

How can I know how his Heaven would be?

At Wuthering Heights *Linton's was so*
different to Cathy's — his calm, sedate,
beatifically still; hers wild, wind-tossed,
restless, with raging grasses' green furnaces
and somersaulting cloud like Vincent's
toiling skies and blasted fields —
moors for a coal-black Borinage...

Perhaps it would be cosseted Datchet,
or adolescent Somerset,
head full with chivalry, untested beliefs,
cushioned in his mother's lap,
his Mammy, our Nana, who appeared
to him the day she passed on, haloed
glowing, smiling, breathless, shining,
for relieving him of bereaving her,
lifting his motherless despair...

...she saved him once before
when he was only four
protecting him with the cover
of her body on the bedroom floor,
shadows of doodlebugs hurtling
like daddy-long-legs off the wall...
... Lily was ground down with scoured stone
an angel on her hands and knees scrubbing
cold stone floors, searching for her nose
she thought had fallen off — in horror

at her face missing in the mirror...
...so many obsessions cobwebbed in
the morbid cottage of her thoughts...
She'd lasted to know one grandson,
witness the birth of a second, cradling
him in her thin, bone china arms,
hushabying under thundering breath...

The dead are everywhere:
in our thoughts, emotions, feelings, faces,
dreams, ideas, and tired love-making,
looks, books, moods, but most of all
our memories — immortality
is true, not just in living genes
but moments of private recollection
of long passed-on loved ones or friends……
until the last human passes on,
most of us — save the lost recluse —
will earn posterity, whether it be
in other peoples' backward looks
or gossamer balm of photo books…

VII Amber Alert

An historic specimen caught in amber
alert, frozen in inertia of time…

> *…Alistair of Histories,*
> *ballasted on nicotine,*
> *he traced ancestors' to their arsenal*
> *of the Past, to make a cast.*
> *Ambered in self-blame for a*
> *family stamped by his bad luck,*
> *he now recludes in smoke-fogged rooms —*
> *a mind's alms-house bricked-in by books,*
> *rug-bound with nostalgias —*
> *drags at tar-stained histories...*

...drawn-out, worn-out sip of tea,
quick drag of singed fag, back on gate,
out in rustic Devonian darkness
of dour doom-laden Dartmoor,
sleep-starved slough of the witching-hour…

...pale-mooned, dim-beamed, patting jumper-arm,
pitter-patting peak-capped purgatory,
outside till half-past late when dawn
yawns and draws the blinds of night
thoughts ticking out of clock-time...
for day to listless-sunbeam in,
bruise the sky with a blow of cloud
till that magic hour, that thought-sedated,
morphine morning pardoning —
he'll stand in the chattering sentry box
by the ink-blotted gate, and wait…

Sounds: guard dogs' salivating pants,
malformed whispers of sleeping trees
hush-a-bye-babying their boughs,
hollow whistling of bitten breeze,
soulless groans of distant cars purring

along staggered lanes, frosty bite
of bitter airs on his crinkled skin…

> — *Can I see your pass?*
> (Silent shoulder-shrug of stranger…)
> — *Then I can't let you through,*
> *Whoever you are, friend or foe,*
> *Can't let you through…*

…those are his orders — note in his book:

> *Man without pass tried to get in.*
> *Refused him. One-Hundred hrs am.*

Who was it? Some wandering Samaritan
wending his spectral wayfare here
to this hubris-blunted man,
to offer him a helping hand
out from this life of nightly trial,
of sleep-starved shifts, of clocking-in,
poorly paid by a private firm
for eight hours' guarding remote and purpling
Naval barracks of red-brick Bickleigh
till ever-receding morning…
…surrounded by blacked-out moors,
looming tors ghostly aglow
like luminous giant grubs in the dark…rough
crags wind-scoured as his torch-lit face…

> *what a lonely empty nothing place this is, this is,*
> *what a lonely empty nothing space this is…*

…space void   oblivion blackness   starlit…
strange lights in the sky…   pinpoints un-
-identified — trying to get to the heart
of the matter, of the blasted atom, just

leads to broken nerves or worse:

o b l i v i o n…

dozing planets...Holst must have turned O
in his orbit when they discovered Pluto

...stars spark faint in vast night sky
like sleepy dust in his bloodshot eye
of yellowed white like a broken egg
splitting into an omelette...
...broken eggs, spilt yoke, spilt milk
of human kindness splitting spitting
tipping pitying down... Two am
drizzle drums to rain, bucketing
down on grounds where soggy dog-ends
gasp out, hiss where mangy guard dogs
piss, sopping his holey boots wet-through,
shuffling about in shadow puddles...
...frozen hob-nailed toes...

...like frost-bitten Scott, Wilson, Bowers,
and martyr 'Titus' Oates opting out
to his frozen immortal legend:
'I may be gone for some time'...or:
'Just answering the call of nature...'
Suicides are rarely spoken,
some are accidental, committed
often in mind, bungled in deed —
mostly without knowing it
we opt for our own oblivions...

...holey-socked frozen toes rub together
resuscitating each others' leather-
skins to thaw in damp-bogged socks...

...stopped clocks' fatigue-defeated thoughts...

...time to drift off...snooze a while — no!
must stay awake — force eye-shutters up —
ungodly hour — just for a few minutes,

half-slumbering mind's brief lie-in,
only kept *compos mentis* by

not being dry, chained to a draughty
chattering sentry box, cold wind-
-creaking vertical coffin, coughing
now, he's coughing…

...slow, tocking, stocking clocks…

Call of duty, early reveille
shoots through shuteye lids
like cold air through a throbbing tooth —
wakes him up with a trumpet-start!

...churning up muck of smoker's cough,
custardy rivulets running in tissues'
arteries… *rain in his tissue-creased face...*
too much fag-fog, nose bunged-up,
chest catarrh-clagged, Corporal's throat
strained from drill and tickling,
no buff lozenges brook the moat
of mucus pouring, better button-up
the top of his tarpaulin coat,
rub shivering hands together stinging
with cold, getting old, had his basinful
of coughing, being out in the cold…

typically bleak West Country weather…

...at the end of his far-stretched tether,
at the end of a shivering cigarette…
Oh to cope, to smoke, to choke, to cope —
Was it circumstance brought the word
'cope' howling into our diction?
What a funny, troubled world it is,
poor relation of its cousin 'hope'
whose absence tends to summon in
through consonantal drift…
its fellow monosyllabic trope

— Father, what's the point to life?
— To cope son, to cope

— But why do we need to cope?
— Why do we need to need?
— But what if we don't cope?
— Then there's always the rope...

O Little Father Time
The box-string snapped your spine
And the babes are hung like dummies —
Now three less empty tummies

His epithet for *being* is *to cope*,
endure (a lesson the services taught him),
such has been his life's burnt purpose —
his special expertise, this connoisseur
of coping, paragon of self-punishing…

An innocent victim of the Furies
O save me from the galloping Furies —
said Swellfoot and Orestes…

Maybe we should each be content
just to be, however we be,
whether well, or insufferably…

There is a special place in Purgatory
reserved for wallowers in self-pity,
thus spake Virgil and Dante…

There's something smothering, powerless
to love, an implacable martyr-streak
that self-crucifies implicitly,
heaps such high self-expectations on
the heart, force-feeds its loved ones
(*...simply too much to grow up to...*)
lumped junkets of interdependency,
clogs their passageways like bronchitis,
weighs on their chests with the heaviness
of spiritual-paralysis, dependence…
(*...suffocating stuff of love...*)

An evangelical peddler said
to a friend of a friend of mine
'Wouldn't it be nice if everyone
in the world loved one another?'
To which my doubting friend of a friend
expressed his growing horror
at such a universal spell:
'No — it would be terrifying
and my idea of Hell...'

...he's spent his life turning his cheek,
forgiving others while trying to seek
their forgiveness, forgiveness from debts,
but forgiveness has no return save itself
so left him bankrupt, sold-short, broke...
seems Good is no longer legal tender...

But how worse would our world be
if Christ hadn't sacrificed his compass-
-ion to save us from our sins?
And preached to love thy neighbour
and turn the other cheek...
beatify the meek...
but remember...

there is a time for breaking down
and a time for building up...

VIII Time for the Nightly Trial

Translated of the Bar quakes up to his place:
ghostly gaunt-faced prosecutor,
skin like curdled junket, cobwebbed
periwig scrolling down his scalp,
his ageless scratchy voice spits out
detritus from the grave, clearing
his organ-bellow chest:

I will draw the jury's attention to those
salient points in my descendant's life;
on the following familial inquisition
I instruct Counsel to advise…

...now turns to his defendant descendant...

— When was your first 'nervous lapse,
for want of a better phrase to sum up
the un-sum-up-able? Or shall we say, sir,
the occasion of your first 'spiritual insight'?

— I was filled-in in a Plymouth man-hole
for being peacemaker, trying to stop
two Bootnecks beating each-other up…

— And the second?

— When Daddy died, whispering in my ear
with ashy breath, in a tone as alone
and distant as the grave, "My son
all I've ever taught you is wrong..."
Put himself up on trial on his deathbed,
thought his bedroom was a courtroom,
dreamt a jury had condemned him shouting
"Guilty! Guilty! Guilty!"
Tough as old boots, straight as laces, Daddy,
formidable horseman, Northumberland
Hussars, battled through Somme, Passchendaele

mud, Flanders fog,   nerves like cheese-wire
only cried when horse fell from under him
death screech drowned   screeching shells
blaze of flares…

— The third insight?

— When Mammy died, felt like world's end,
everything to me, my sun and rain,
I remember her gently tinkling
on our piano, 'Rustle of Spring'…
Mammy, my breakfast, tea time, warmth,
my faith, my mental snugness, my
self-esteem, my love of life…

— Until?

— Helen Parker claimed my heart...
my twenty-fourth summer when I first saw her,
smartly pressed in my full dress
on that airless train clattering back
from barracks to cob-toothed Seaton,
Catholic schoolgirl, uniformed
in chocolate-brown with mustard piping,
a thornless rose in her fifteenth bloom;
her laughter light as summer balm…

— Did this sunnier insight last?

— A year on from that first train journey
punished for loving her: possessive mother
garbled her mind against me…

— Hence your third dead-end?

— Yes, but Daddy sorted it out,
spoke up to her parents, shifted the cloud,
soon after we married, for better, for worse,
for richer, for poorer…
— Which brings us neatly…

— Which brings us neatly…

— Betrayal: my ex-best man, best friend,
best Bootneck mate (nicknamed me Fred)
brought me down to a low I've yet
to clamber from…an over-stressed
commuter, fled Big Smoke, bomb threats,
rush hours, rank air, tautened breaths,
with my wife, two sons, took up his offer
of a Cornish cottage in idyllic village,
a gnarled-faced house, old stones and slates —
desk job in his building business…

— How did the next storm come?

Bankruptcy ruined him so he ruined me,
thrown into oblivion of poverty,
debt, depression, unemployment,
black sense of failure that wouldn't lift —
forced to go for any job I could get,
flog old family heirlooms (while I
flogged myself in my private mind):
my brother's ormolu cabinet,
the Chippendale table with a chip in it,
had to pawn my wife's gold wedding ring
scrimp and save almost anything,
polish old mouldy copper coins,
haunt car-boot sales with our sons' old toys…

— I perceive the jury wishes to adjourn...

...his sons, like those two guiding the horse
of their sightless king in that saffron-foxed
old book…

I see him stone-still, prayer-clasped
hands, a granite gauge-hound at his feet,
mother peaceful beside him, both
in perpetual instatement they'd never
known in life — a knight who knew
no reinstatement: permanent

in repose as a last sculpted gesture,
Plantagenet-nosed in quixotic armour

...the eldest, bullied at school
but too proud and introverted to voice
it aloud…kept his pain to himself upstairs,
shut up in his room studying...
...downstairs,
the youngest sucked his thumb, cocooned
in a filthy sleeping bag, pampered,
homebirdish, suffering love, powerless
to express his jumbled-up mind, absent
from school, falling far behind…suffering…
love… powerless… suffer….

...starve and suffer, go without warmth,
freeze and sneeze in dusty damp beds, wear
second-hand clothes, bear second-hand breaths,
hear asthmatic sons wheezing in damp nights,
pull blankets over his despairing eyes…
wish to be dead and forgiven…
(not existing but forgotten…)

...wish for nothing save peace of mind,
for someone to rid of him of the lease
of this tumbled stone nadir that served
as home, where no one visited...
(*their own little House of Usher*
crumbling symbiotically around them)
...no post arrived, save red reminders
and repossession threats;
interminable chain-mail of debts…

A face peered through the two-way window
of our shadow-cottage; squinting in
with sun-shade hand, he shook back as
the dogs claw-scraped up to the ledge,
barking ferociously as Cerberus
at the gates of Hades; I, Orpheus
with my shrinking father quickly stirred
as if discovered in a rustic squat;

the limbo we shades haunted —
'I'm sorry' called the trespasser
through the starved glass gingerly
retreating, 'I didn't think this house
was inhabited' — and nor did we...

...in-between a morass of number-littered
papers heaped on his listing desk
doubts piling his obsessing brow,
worried fingers punch at buttons
of a faulty plastic calculator,
deducts outgoings from his pauper's pay,
joints of his cellotaped NHS glasses
slowly unhinging away…

For me, the sound of Purgatory:
the creak of my father's fingers
fumbling through card files of bills
where warped ambition lingers...

...barely one penny to rub together,
forage for coppers in the nether
glooms beneath the torn settee,
some washing-up liquid to scrub old tender,
bit of brush-scrub, spit and polish —
Will he come through it? Heads or tails?
Hunched in the dark dog-ending away,
nibbles his half-bitten nails…

so little means, so much to pay…

...outgoings, outpourings, occasional outings
to wisteria-crawled mansions, courtesy
of National Trust coupons cut out from
empty tattered tea-bag packets
of under-fed caffeine addicts…

...we all have our vices, even the meek
smoke cigarettes they must eke
like meals for the slaving seven day week,
these shabby genteels in their down-at-heels,

so weak a feeling to live on this diet,
weak as twice-drained tea bags…

Some instructions for the meek:
simply turn the other cheek
& if you've used up both bruised cheeks
& there's no more left to turn
just maybe it is time   to learn...

The Good go unguided, unappreciated,
forgotten, overlooked, ignored, mistaken
for weak-willed, ineffectual, self-pitying,
chippie, pitiful, worse still for the downtrodden
good: no one can fathom or tolerate
the visible victim of arbitrary fate
trampled underfoot by hardship's hooves,
who tries to stand up but is knocked back down
through no fault of his own, nor his shoes —
no one can sympathise with this man
who turns the other cheek from those
who strike him down to powerless throes
of poverty with unprovoked blows…
...no one, because no one wants to think
anyone's poor through no fault of their own;
then it might make them change their views
when they see society only lets them choose
not to put on someone-else's shoes..
Seems all we have the power to choose
are our views… while our votes are transfused
from purpled reds to gerrymandered blues...

It's enough to make you want to tear it all down
but the rebel without a clause, the clown,
the left-wing thinker, all down the pan:
this is the age of the anxious young man…

...scuff of cold split-open shoes
stamps out hissing fag-butt — wrist-
-watch crutches to half-past two…

IX Last Lag of Flagging Nostalgia till Dawn

Tired eyes read same line again.
Time to fold back the top of the page
think on his mother's side again:
the Asgills, thinkers, pink-gin tippling,
respectable, bespectacled intellectuals
with a turn-of-the-century Fabian glow…

…who foresaw walls come tumbling down
through subversiveness of patience
waiting for the time of the system's
suicide, as their namesake Fabius
(as long as no hair spills in with the milk
from the milky hairshirts of their ilk)…

Revolution — just as likely to come
with tea parties as with a gun…

Charitably Baptist, Pelagian, well-read,
March Hared, Mad-Hattering nattering chattering
crockery-clattering Bloomsburystyle,
well-heeled, clean-cuffed, clear thinking minds
receptive to new, untested ideas…

(My great grandfather, the Fabian,
never missed a single meeting
to discuss best ways of feeding
empty bellies of the down-at-heel.
Privately he ate his meals
in his study, apart from his kin:
he couldn't stand the sound
of other people eating.)

…tipsy on empathy, rosy Socialism,
armchair antimacassar Salvationism
in William Morris-wallpapered rooms,
milk-skinned sincerity, pristine white
as porcelain vases by Pre-Raphaelite

firesides; crested tea spoons, silver
service, chink of china tea-things,
clink and clank of antique crockery,
genteel but not at all shabbily, tea-
weaned on compassionate cant of seminal
left-wing supplements' apostolic argot,
taking the New Testament literally:
Give to the poor and thou shalt be free —
So, well-heeled hands together for prayer:

> *Keir Hardie, Aneurin Bevan,*
> *Will Crooks, be thy names,*
> *Thy Clause Four come, thy bill be won,*
> *In the party as it is in Parliament,*
> *Give us this day our daily Left*
> *Forgive us our desperateness*
> *As we forgive those who campaign*
> *against us,*
> *Lead us not into dissention,*
> *But deliver us from Gaitskell,*
> *James Ramsay MacDonald*
> *And the Power of the Tory,*
> *Forever and ever,*
>
> *A. Clem.*

Forgive us our debtors as we forgive those
who debt against us — forgive them, forget them,
forget ourselves, their self-obscured motto
indelibly etched in his mind's Asgillite —
sui oblitus commodi (forgetful
of one's own interests — whatever they
may be…) scrolls altruistically
beneath the crest of a riddling Sphinx…

> *Q: I say, I say, I say:*
> *What creature goes on four legs in the morning;*
> *Two legs during the day*
> *And three legs in the evening?*

A: The worker who begs on all fours for a job;
Gets up onto two to paw for his pay;
And limps with a stick when forced into leaving.

Socialism (now there's a thing —
partly of nostalgia
as well as wishful thinking);
requires too much concentration,
and doesn't work, apparently.
Capitalism? Unquestionably,
at least for the majority,
after all those dispossessed
aren't worth accounting for anyway...

...are they?

All men are equal, his Dad used to say,
But some are more equal than others —
Are they?

(His father took a horsewhip to his arse
when he asked him if he was working-class)

'My country right or wrong' rang hollow
from the pipe-propped mouth of patriotic pater,
a splinter of rhetoric lodged in him
like a papery Kipling battle scar;
but a compassionate patriarch of private
rapture far above the camouflage
of his khaki allegiances;
gutsy, brave, didn't hold with the swank
of officers' messes — and never drank
since his dram-sated father sank
into the dry-house of the grave;
a sober teetotaller of emotion
strapped doubts' shadows in his tunic:
so no stomach for Sassoon, bassoon
or wind of his son's 'guts-ache' music,
Walton/R.V.W./Holst...

His kind have waited languorous-long
for that clank of the letter-box for *News
from Anywhere*, Utopia, parousia... .

*..dig up those Diggers' digs and clod
in England's mean, unpleasant sod…*

*The People sold their Prophet for Profit.
Who would have thought it?
Who could have stopped it?*

*Socialism is now a Dodoism
like love and truth and idealism —
for we have lost our vision…*

Dodos, flamingos, he remembers pink
flamingos spinning before his eyes
when beaten up outside a Plymouth pub
playing 'Pretty Flamingo'…

*God, dear God, why make us believe
The Left is in the right / That only Love is Might
When it has a massive clumsy body
And wings too small for flight?*

*Especially the left-wing.
Left, right, left, right,
Who is wrong, who is right?
About turn…quick march…*

O for wings! If he's a Daedalus
lost in his Labyrinth of self-blame
let me be his Icarus aflame
to burn out before I suffer the same
in all but name — the churning plough
of stone-betrayed and trusting traits
must be obviated somehow…
I'm falling into his martyred trap already:
it's just too easy and uninspired to be bad and
I've always favoured the path of most difficulty…

so resolve to grow old and childless, this is
no world to bring innocents into to be
corrupted by gain or bitterness of loss...

...better be a Tickie: make your own cross
to bear, sacrifice and damn yourself
for love of God.

..there is no colour grey,
only innocence twisted
or so some say...

There's a time for building up
and a time for knocking down...
There's a time for nailing up
and a time for chopping down...

But what of the family name if his sons
don't sow their cautious seeds?
What will be left for us but wills left to charities,
empty deeds, old heirlooms idling in the
indifference of other peoples' rooms
blind to their inanimate sentiments
(*their untapped animism...*)
buried with us in unvisited tombs?
Or anonymous crematoriums
where our scattered ashes fade
on unmarked grass in the unmarked shade
of trees without tributes...

there must be something more therefore

...this my father clings to
as he shivers imperceptibly
like a well-disciplined sentry,
sighs and coughs as his watch shows
the time is Half-Past Three...
Not time to think on ancestry...
Time to build on hobbyish thoughts,
to stimulate the mind out from torpor...

little Hobbit Bilbo Bag-eyes
without his gnarled Gandalf , nor Samwise —

… his only hobbies, heraldry, and tirelessly
tracing back the family tree…

gules moon rampant
sable sky turns azure…

Time to kill, so much time to kill,
time to kill time but what of time lost?
Time stolen? Time gone?...
(*there is a time for killing time...*)
...vapours of fog envelop him once more;
mists of clock-time, clear, reveal
a ghost of ancestral past…

Translated Asgill is conjured again
like a Genie from an uncorked bottle,
dusts off his cobwebbed chamber clothes,
pontificates in cascading wig,
snorts some snuff, splutters up dust,
then vanishes to just his scrolling wig
swallowed by early hour fog...
his humbled descendant continues his slog
through to the next slothful hour…

...about this time
some are snoring in snug beds
some are busy dreaming dreams
some are making love
some are still up talking
some are sinking pints
some are lighting fags
out in the pouring rain
enduring the cold,
the time, the strain…

X Dream Reveille

Four Hundred hrs am. Amen:
only an hour to go till he
can clock-out, soldier home…

...homecoming once had the cheddar-red
yeoman fireside painting about it:
dogs' tails thumping on the carpet,
a father freshly thawed sniffing in
cigarette symbiotic with fingers,
face mapped hardship-shaped —
here was home, bare but warm,
austere but kind, shivers of love
huddling up to a bright fireside...

…now home to damp, cold-water-bottle-
-bed with one warm patch in it:
the impression his wife has left who's traipsed
out down the ragged verge of the dark
downhill road to clock-on for Seven
till her punishment finishes at Two pm...
Post-Meridian — post-exhaustion....

That morosely comforting homely picture
still distant in his dreamful mind
notices his watch still tells the same time…

...old clock stutters its welcoming, the
lounge ghost sighs out stale oat-breath
interpreted as a draught. The dogs
sit expectant, frisky tails fanning
the air, whine and fuss for exercise,
snort and gabble, scuttle and skid
on peeling lino, scratching patches
of concrete on the kitchen floor —
their food is cold but they want more
to barter over; to annexe off...

or maybe it's stopped? No such luck,
fat chance, — the second-hand plods
the deceptive distance,
of a whole wilderness-like minute.
Sneezes and wheezes and sneezes.
Time makes its own limits,
passes as fast as it pleases…
...blows his nose in over-used hanky,
then in a used tissue emaciated
as an excavator's stringy find;
sucks on a mint to the knock of his teeth,
at Half-Past Four sighs with relief:
time for another tea-break...

...summoned by their master's cough
and incitement of jangling leads, they
paw and scrap in mad anticipation
at the battered wood front door,
cabin-fevered pining for space,
panting scrape and scarper of paw…

Hopefully his mess-fellows aren't so awake
to use up his precious reading time
gassing on anything coming to mind,
interminable itineraries: dodgy health,
houses, motors, sexual stealth,
wives and satellites, tabloids, soaps,
and whatever other nullities help
these beer-bellied Behemoths cope…

Topics of the more myopic of optics…

...empty kettles
hissing away
until the steam settles
whistling as they come to the boil...

— Fill it up Al,
coffee, black, two sugars, there's a pal!

Cloud of steam settles, cups filled up,
topped up, supped up, washed up, back out-
-side a bit more warmed up, kept semi-
conscious with tea and nicotine,
ventilated with a mint, hovering
up to five 'o' clock, last lag of the shift…

but O such a slothful one…
the formless foggy final slog
to the magic six 'o' clock…

...dawn's approaching, off horizon,
yawning amber spills from fading night,
tea pouring out on a table-cloth sky,
past distant hills, barely in sight,
pouring over the bleak and brooding
moors, promising day, the sun that shines
(*that he wishes were the Downs...*)
on all, from the biggest builder to
the most expendable tool…
...the dawning, yawning, morning hour
usurps the night, re-forms the day,
grants its pale endurers eight
hours' worth of serf-like pay…
clocked-up for the dead-end of the month,
already spoken for by arrears…

...if he has to have his time again he prays
for a different path to this hard-travelled one;
at Saxon-dipthonged Æthelmar,
and Curry Mallet's homely Rector
Dynevor Rees-Jones, to follow a more
pastoral path — not his father's advice
into the forces, or his later instincts
to default for the Civil Service,
a commuting, sighing, pin-striped Perrin —
but he'd be that rural parish vicar
he was suited to be...(not a Born Again
new-fangled type like that Landrake Vicar
and his kith who tried to convert his Catholic

wife and recusant sons to anathema
and excommunication, through
hamper alms that mysteriously arrived
left on the doorstep, silent as faith
as if these benefactors were ashamed
of their unfashionable compassion…)

In the creel of a slate-skied Cornish winter
we caught a scraping sound outside;
a huge mass landing, heavy as the weight
my father prayed would be lifted from
his jobless shoulders scraped and bowed —
cold wind shot through the hallway, lo!
we beheld a hamper packed with tins
and vegetables — no Christians,
just a scribbled note blown on the lino
saying 'from the Parish' — my father scowled:
now he was obliged to let them Save him...

...but a studious, reflective life in which
his unsung strengths would best have been
employed, his fellow man best served,
To Serve Them All His Days in quiet
dorms, uninterrupted studies
surrounded by his history books,
genealogical charts, and Vaughan
Williams' records, slow tock of clocks,
not sat hunched at a makeshift desk
in a flown son's cramped abandoned bedroom,
huddled over bills, eyes traipsing
the slog of the tripping clock,
haunted infinitum by Nine pm,
just time for a flustered lukewarm
shower, blacking scrub of boot-
polish thoughts on giving in,
clocking-out to clock back in
half a day later…
that old 'quick swing'…
half a pay later
half a life
later

seisactheia I sigh!

...he prays God's merciful next time:
offers him respite from this grind,
this term existing instead of living,
no peace of death, just wakeful haunting
himself for infinity, a shadow
of his former stride, a life-haunting
shade for only having haunted life...
...spare me, he thinks, *from a same fate recurring,*
offer me a new beginning
on level ground where we all have power
to choose our course, no servitude
of clocking-in for the witching-hour...

XI Release

Six Hundred hours Amen.
All men
are free to clock-out
snail back home
in muttering cars
down empty roads
to beds warmed by
impressions of wives —
sink into pillows
for six blessed hours,
dream better shifts
than punished lives…

Acknowledgements

An earlier draft of 'Keir Hardie Street' was published in *The Mansion Gardens* (Paula Brown, 2006). I would like to thank the following for their encouragement regarding this work: Paula Brown, John O'Donoghue, Simon Jenner, Sebastian Barker, Barry Tebb; as well as the following critics for their encouraging reviews of its earlier version: Gwilym Williams, William Oxley, Stephanie Smith-Browne and Michael W. Thomas. Thanks most of all to Andy Croft for commissioning a redrafted version of the poem for publication under the Smokestack imprint, which is for me its natural home.

'Clocking-in for the Witching Hour' was originally published in a slightly shorter form as a limited edition pamphlet by Sixties Press in 2004. It received some enthusiastic critical notice at the time, from Stephanie Smith-Browne, Graham High and the late Martin Blyth. I thank them all for their early encouragement regarding this work; also Simon Jenner, for his painstaking assistance with the earliest edit of the piece; and Barry Tebb for being the first to champion the work. The end section of the poem, 'Release', was included in *Night Shift* (Five Leaves Publications, 2010; Michael Baron, Andy Croft and Jenny Swann (eds)).